A powerful, heartfelt and inspiring memoir from one of Australia's leading human rights advocates, Kon Karapanagiotidis, *The Power of Hope* tells the story of how Kon overcame his traumatic childhood of racism, bullying and loneliness to create one of Australia's largest and best-loved human rights organisations, the Asylum Seeker Resource Centre, which has gone on to transform the lives of thousands of refugees and has helped build a movement.

A book about how love, compassion, kindness and courage can transform our communities and ourselves, *The Power of Hope* shows us in times of darkness, both personal and political, that if we stand as one we can shine brightly and fiercely – as together, we are powerful.

Kon Karapanagiotidis is the CEO and founder of the Asylum Seeker Resource Centre, the largest independent human rights organisation for refugees and people seeking asylum in Australia. It assists thousands of people each year, with the help of over 1,200 volunteers and 125 staff.

Kon grew up in a working-class family in a small country town in Victoria. His personal experience of racism and witnessing the exploitation of his parents in factories and farms planted the seeds of his passion for human rights. He started volunteering at a centre for homeless men at the age of 18, and went on to do volunteer work at 24 other charities. He also completed 6 degrees, becoming a lawyer, social worker, and teacher. Kon founded the ASRC at the age of 28.

His work has been recognised with over two dozen awards and honours, including an Order of Australia Medal (OAM) and a Churchill Fellowship. He was a finalist for Australian of The Year (Victoria) and the Human Rights Medal, as well as Citizen of the Year in his local community.

THE POWER OF HOPE

The Power of Hope

Kon Karapanagiotidis

HarperCollins*Publishers*

HarperCollins*Publishers*
Australia • Brazil • Canada • France • Germany • Holland • India
Italy • Japan • Mexico • New Zealand • Poland • Spain • Sweden
Switzerland • United Kingdom • United States of America

HarperCollins acknowledges the Traditional Custodians of the land upon which we live and work, and pays respect to Elders past and present.

First published on Gadigal Country in Australia in 2018
This edition published in 2024
by HarperCollins*Publishers* Australia Pty Limited
ABN 36 009 913 517
harpercollins.com.au

A catalogue record for this book is available from the National Library of Australia

ISBN 978 1 4607 6747 4 (paperback)
ISBN 978 1 4607 0949 8 (ebook)
ISBN 978 1 4607 9769 3 (audio)

Cover design and internal design by Hazel Lam, HarperCollins Design Studio
Author photograph by Kim Landy
Typeset by Kirby Jones
Printed and bound in Australia by McPherson's Printing Group

IN MEMORY OF MY FATHER, LEO,
AND FOR MY MUM, SIA, AND MY SISTER, NOLA.

THERE IS NO ME WITHOUT ANY OF YOU AND
YOUR SACRIFICES AND ENDURING LOVE.

CONTENTS

HOW THINGS CAN CHANGE

PROLOGUE

It's midnight on a wintry West Melbourne evening in 2007. My sister, Nola, and I have just spilt out of the Asylum Seeker Resource Centre's purple building and onto Jeffcott Street. The mosque across the road that always welcomes us is closed. We walk towards King Street, the beautiful Flagstaff Gardens – Wurundjeri land – now in sight and shining in the wet light. But even this, remarkably, is unable to lift my spirits.

I'm feeling stuck.

'What's the point?' I ask Nola. 'Are we making any difference at all? It all feels so futile. This government is just crushing refugees and what we do doesn't matter.' I sigh heavily. 'I feel so powerless. I just don't know if I can keep doing this.'

I've been working since 9 am, which is pretty standard. For my first seventeen years running the Asylum Seeker

Resource Centre (ASRC) a seventy- or eighty-hour week was the norm, so that isn't what's bothering me. I'm feeling broken after yet another bruising Wednesday-night legal clinic. Sure, one family had been granted asylum and rejoiced with tears of joy after years of struggle, and a dozen other families had their initial asylum claims lodged so they were full of hope. But I had spent most of the night telling people that their claims for asylum had been refused, that their legal options had been exhausted and they would have to prepare to return to their home country. As a human rights lawyer I have had this conversation with refugees many hundreds of times over the last seventeen years. And each and every time the response is the same – total and absolute devastation.

I have had people collapse in front of me, while others weep uncontrollably. Of course I try my best to comfort and counsel them. And I've had others who have threatened to kill themselves on hearing such bad news. I keep those people from leaving my office until I have a safety and care plan in place for them. One night I kicked in the front door of a refugee's home fearing they were going to take an overdose to kill themselves. And another time I had a refugee slash his arm in front of me in a moment of total despair and I had to stop him bleeding to death right there and then.

It's difficult for everyday Australians to understand the grief and loss in this crippling moment when refugees hear such bad news. They have crossed half the earth in search of freedom, escaping lives torn apart by civil war, oppression and tyranny. Many of the people I have to speak to are fathers – they came first, often taking the perilous journey by sea so their families wouldn't have to. They came to establish a new life before sending for their loved ones. These brave fathers have missed so many firsts: first birthdays, first baby steps, first words, first wedding anniversaries and the first place they called home.

These men have spent anywhere from two to ten years to get to this point and are then told it's over. Some of them survived years in immigration prisons, years of being denied the right to work or to study. They've had their mental and physical health ripped apart from the anxiety and depression caused by years of limbo, only to be told it's finally over.

This is why I'm feeling broken. Even though I know I've done all I can, it's just me in that room with them and I'm tearing their dreams apart.

Enough of the walking.

I step out into the road to hail an approaching cab. It's late, we should be home. The cab driver says hello and Nola and I slump into the back, both relieved that sleep isn't far away.

The driver is staring at me in the rear-view mirror.

'Do you remember me, Kon?' he asks. He turns around in his seat to speak to me face to face. 'You helped me years ago when my family and I first arrived in Australia. You were my lawyer and helped us get asylum. And then,' he says with a smile and shake of his head, 'once we had somewhere to live, you and your friend Pablo turned up with a truckload of furniture to fill our home. We'd been sleeping on the floor before that.'

And now I recognise his face. It's Mohamed. He came from Iraq. We shake hands, and he turns back to the road and starts driving. We talk and laugh, and he tells me how well his family is doing now.

When we pull up to my house Mohamed refuses to take any money. 'Please, this is the least that I can do for you,' he says and grips my hand with both of his. It is a fond farewell and his last words hit home: 'I will never forget what you've done. You saved my family and I will always be indebted to you.'

That chance encounter has stayed with me and it has nourished me ever since. I don't know what the odds of something like that happening that night are, all I know is how much it meant to me and how much I needed to hear those words. It reminded me that you can make a difference to the lives of people even when you don't realise it. It reminded me of my own vocation. It reminded me of the power that hope can bring, and it reminded me that we have to keep helping and we have to keep fighting, for all our sakes.

IT REMINDED ME OF THE POWER THAT HOPE CAN BRING, AND IT REMINDED ME THAT WE HAVE TO KEEP HELPING AND WE HAVE TO KEEP FIGHTING, FOR ALL OUR SAKES.

1

FAMILY

We all have stories to tell and mine begins with my grandmother Parthena. I remember her hands, which carried the deep scars of sacrifice and the heaviness of time and of great loss. Yet her hands were as strong as they were worn. Zeus would have worshipped them. To me my *yiayia* was a hero, a lioness who protected her family at all costs. She raised seven children with love and determination, and my father, Leo, was one of them. She was one of the hundreds of thousands of Greeks caught up in the Pontic Genocide, which lasted for nearly ten years, ending in 1923. This form of ethnic cleansing was sanctioned by the government of the Ottoman Empire, and included massacres, forced deportations (often to death camps) and the attempted wholesale destruction of Greek culture. So my *yiayia*'s sacrifices and losses were all bound up with having been forced from her homeland. She was a refugee who had to start her life over again in a new home. She married and raised her family in the village of Apsilo, a town of a few thousand in the mountains of northern Greece. The most important thing to her was family, and she spent all her days doing everything she possibly could to give her children a better life.

I visited Apsilo when I was ten years old and slept in the modest, faded Greek-blue home where my father was born and raised. I remember the barren fields, now no longer fertile, where my father had worked from the age of nine. I remember meeting his three beautiful sisters, the same ones he ploughed the fields for so that they could have a wedding dowry and improve their futures. And to this day I try to imagine how my father felt in the early 1940s when, at the age of only five, Nazis marched into his village and took control. How terrifying these strange men with their uniforms and weapons must have been for him. It was something he never forgot.

No migrant parent ever wants their child to leave the family home, but my grandparents (like so many others) sent my father to Australia when he was twenty-six years old. Their hopes were that he would be free of poverty, and that he could create the future he wanted and they were unable to give him. Here was a chance for their son not to have to go without all the time or with so little. I often think of what that moment must have been like for my

My father with his parents in his hometown in Greece.

grandmother, saying goodbye to her young Leo, knowing she might never see him or hold him again. For those of us with migrant backgrounds, it is extraordinary what our parents, grandparents or great-grandparents sacrificed to give us this new life in Australia.

And the story of migrants and refugees, our collective story, is what is entirely missing from the national conversation on immigration. The cold, hard truth is that people really don't want to leave their homes unless they have to. They don't want to say goodbye to their family, community, culture and friends, and to start all over again in a foreign land where so often they are greeted with suspicion, racism and resistance.

My 'uneducated' parents came to Australia without a word of English and went on to raise two children who between them would hold eight university degrees and an Order of Australia medal, and who would both receive acclaim and recognition in their legal professions and human rights. My parents sacrificed everything for Nola and me, working as labourers on farms and in factories until their bodies could no longer take it. They worked hard for more than forty years so that their children could dream of something better. All of it was for us. They had no lives outside of us. They were driven by the most profound love, and the determination that we would have a better life than them at any cost to themselves.

'I don't want anyone to speak to you or treat you the way I am treated every day,' my parents would tell me. To this day I still struggle to understand the magnitude of their sacrifices. I am still yet to be a father (though I do hope to be, one day), so it's difficult for me to understand fully why they did what they did for us, but what I do know is that without the sacrifices my parents made I wouldn't have this life at all. There would probably be no degrees, no being a public figure, no boundless choices, no chance to do what I dreamed of, or to create something from scratch, which is what I love so much about the ASRC. Instead, I'd most likely be standing in an assembly line in a factory somewhere.

I am able to reach for the stars and touch the sky because I was on their shoulders. They held me up. They endured years of 4 am starts, working days that finished long after dinnertime, and work on weekends. They had no travel or holidays, no thoughts of a sea change, just endless sacrifices by the two of them for my sister and me.

And through the very act of their doing, my parents taught me things that no formal school education can – they taught me about resilience, the importance of family, principles, sacrifice, entrepreneurship, selflessness and courage. That's in my DNA, and it's in the blood of every single migrant and refugee who sets foot on this land.

I know I simply won the lottery of time and place. Around a century ago my grandmother fled her homeland as a refugee; seventy-five years ago my father grew up with the Nazis occupying his little country town, and a few years after that began working in the fields for his family. I understand in many ways that my privilege, my freedom, my choices and safety are little more than the luck of time and place. This is what is so often forgotten in the debate about refugees, that it's just a birthright lottery and nothing more. That desperate father, mum and child on a leaky boat washing up on our shores could be us, our dads, mums and sisters, our grandmas. What would we want for them? I know for me it would be the hand of compassion, the embrace of welcome, the bridge of friendship and love to be extended to my family.

My dad had such a way with people he could make a stranger trust him in a moment – that was his charm. I used to watch him both in confusion and awe, going with him to the bottle shop between paydays and getting a slab to take home just with the assurance he would pay them the next week. And I saw him do the same with boarding buses and getting groceries. Imagine trying to do that at Coles! People trusted my dad because he was a man of his word. He even insisted on paying interest on anything that was given to him on trust, even if it was only a dollar. It was the principle that mattered to him.

When Nola and I were young kids we lived in the country, and both Mum and Dad worked on tobacco farms before we moved to Melbourne, where they took up work in factories. Menial labour was not something Dad had wanted for himself. Several times a year, every year, my father would tell me the story of how his teacher had begged his parents not to take him out of school at the age of nine to work in the fields. 'Leo could be anything,' he had said to them, 'a doctor or a lawyer, if he could just stay in school.' But that was the last year of schooling he would ever have. Dad never told me this story with any anger but always with a keen sense of sadness. He wanted to make sure I knew that he had always wanted something better for himself than a life knee-deep in shitty tobacco farms or asbestos-filled factories. He wanted me to know that he could have been *somebody*. But he always was to me, and I wish I'd told him.

Something I found so very special about my dad was his way of finding beauty in the most unexpected places. Once we moved to Melbourne he cleared an area around a barren, filthy wool-dye factory in Collingwood and planted a wonderful garden. It was his oasis, his refuge, his place of beauty – something that he had created and that gave him not only peace and a space to reflect in safety, but also the pleasure of having made something from nothing, and, even more practically, that provided homegrown vegetables. He loved his garden and it was his sanctuary from home and work, his place of peace and wonder.

None of this is to say that my dad was an easy man to get along with most of the time. Like many men, particularly of that generation, he was reticent and found it difficult to show his feelings. And he was also deeply affected by his childhood years and the struggles he had borne. I can't help but think that my father never had a chance at happiness, never had a chance to be the man he dreamed of being and would have been, and that had been denied him because of the ravages of poverty and the shadows of war. His was a generation that would have no childhood and that would see few dreams realised.

My dad died at the age of sixty-three after fifty-two years of endless toil on farms and in factories. I had made him retire at sixty-one so that my sister and I could look after him for a change, but he was dead within two years. My sorrow and bitterness at his early death won't ever leave me.

What had happened was that after saving for ages I sent Mum and Dad to Greece for a three-month holiday. My dad hadn't seen his parents and three sisters in fifteen years and I had thought no one should be apart from their family for so long. My dad, so humble, so selfless, never dreamed of buying a ticket to go home himself, because we – his kids – always came first. But I had remembered the day we left Apsilo after a visit when I was ten. My dad once again had to say goodbye to his mother, and the sorrow in her eyes and the disbelief at losing her son all over again was heartbreaking. This was her only son whom she had never wanted to give up in the first place.

I remember hugging my dad goodbye at Melbourne Airport departures. It's always a busy part of the airport with family members bidding each other farewell. I had somewhat brazenly stepped over into the 'Do Not Enter' area to say goodbye better. We gave each other a long, hard hug. I can still remember his arms around me. I told him I loved him. I am so thankful that I did. It was the last time I saw my father alive.

Ten days before he was due to fly home from his three-month holiday, my father died of a sudden heart attack. He died in the middle of the night, in my mum's little Greek village where she had been raised. I still grieve for him every day. To be honest, it has taken me years to get over feeling like I had personally killed him. I have spent years blaming myself with 'if onlys'. If only I had not sent him to Greece, if only he had been here in Australia when it happened I could have saved him. If he had been here we would have called an ambulance and got him to a good hospital in time. If only that had happened, he would still be with us right now. To this day I still don't know what to do with the guilt I feel from this. I try to keep perspective, reminding myself that I couldn't possibly have known this would happen, but still the 'if onlys' persist.

Now, with the benefit of time having passed, of course a part of me is grateful that Dad died in his homeland, that he had the chance to see and reconnect with his family one more time, especially after not having been back there for so very long. But it was terribly painful for the entire family when it came to bringing him home – his sisters wanted him buried in his hometown so they could be near him at all times, but I could not imagine how we would manage with him so far away from us and we brought him home. I can still see my poor mum the day she and Dad left for Greece, smiling and hugging me and Nola at the airport, and then, just a couple of months later, she returned home a widow, alone, her husband of twenty-five years gone forever.

I want to remember my father in his prime, driving his cool, white Chrysler Valiant (the same one I was embarrassed to be seen in as a kid), wearing his cherry-red shirt with the collar way up and the shirt buttoned low to show off his hairy chest and six-pack. My dad was so handsome; in his classic blue jeans with the bottoms rolled up and well-worn Blundstones, he looked like a leading man of a bygone era, someone worthy of a John Ford film perhaps. And I have a photo that captures this leading man from times past so well. In it Dad looks rather like a

Greek Clint Eastwood with sideburns. He has a cigarette dangling from the fingers of one hand and an arm lovingly slung around the shoulders of my mum, who is in her best summer dress with a beehive hairdo, looking so glam, with the Australian Alps in the background. This is the photo of my parents I love the most. When I look at it I imagine two lovers, and two friends, where life is theirs for the taking. I imagine that their potential will be lived in their own lifetimes, and not only through me and my sister. I feel so much sorrow that they were both cheated of their summer love. I know my mother's dress was rarely worn after that shining day. What do you do with a lifetime of hurt that can't heal?

Grief can be so corrosive, especially when it's accompanied by regret. It's my experience that regret takes away forgiveness, perspective and history and just leaves you with all of the pain and little else, apart, perhaps, from the exhausting fantasy that you tirelessly play out in your head of what you would have said or should have said or could have done. Clearly that's destructive behaviour when the reality is that you just did the best you could at the time, no matter how shitty that might have been.

I work on that forgiveness with each year that passes, but even after so many years I still don't have the solace or perspective I need – I don't know if I ever will – but I will keep trying.

GRIEF IS ALSO A PART OF LOVE. THIS IS ONE REASON WE FEEL IT SO DEEPLY AND KEENLY.

I know there are families where the damage inflicted on members has been so great there may be no chance of healing, but if you have had arguments or stand-offs with your family and are currently estranged, I urge you now to reach out to them. I know from personal experience that once they are gone all you are left with is regret. Let go of the anger. Let go of being right. Let go of not wanting to be the one who makes the first move. When they are gone that's it, and you will regret what you left unhealed and unspoken. Grief is also a part of love. This is one reason we feel it so deeply and keenly. We grieve for those things we love and have lost, and that's why we hold onto it for so long.

My mum, Sia, is a force of nature. No one has loved me more and yet at the same time created so many issues for me. She had such an unforgiving childhood. Like my father she was forced to leave school at an early age, in her case she was twelve. My mother grew up in poverty, the youngest of four children, with little freedom and fewer choices. Her authoritarian father wanted her to avoid the life of poverty he had to endure, at any cost. There is more than a little irony to this, because it turns out my grandmother had come from a wealthy family and once she had made the decision to marry for love and had married my grandfather, her family disowned her.

Then of course the repercussions of having to live with this decision became much clearer to her. In fact, my grandmother used to warn my mother that if ever a boy approached her to start a conversation she should run, run for her dear life! It breaks my heart knowing that. So my mum's father decided that she would move to Australia and make a start on a better life, one free from poverty. It's strange to think how Mum had no control over any part of her life, including moving to the other side of the world, and all at the tender age of twenty.

I truly believe my mum could have been anything. She has limitless energy and reserves of strength and to this day she can still do the work of ten men. Aside from my father, I have never seen anyone with a stronger work ethic. She worked in farms and factories until her body was broken, and yet continued on long past these jobs to do whatever it took to care for her family – and she still does to this day. If she had been born in a different time I have no doubt her tenacity and industry would have seen her play a role in the Senate, or as a CEO or perhaps even a Supreme Court judge. My mum, too, like my father and grandmother, had simply lost the lottery of time and place.

Sia had such big dreams and hopes when she came to Australia. And like my father she dedicated herself to feeding and raising her children so they could become something. None of her own ambitions for herself were realised. My mum tells me she was top of her class in Maths and had dreamt of being a Maths teacher. But her mum was sick and her father needed help on the farm so, like my father, she had to abandon her dreams for her family's sake. She felt so alone in a country where she never truly felt welcome, and yet she knew she could have been more and done so much more.

No one loves me more deeply than my mother and no one ever will, but the disappointment and grief she was burdened with also became my grief to help carry for her, which as a son you do. And I tried very hard to do that, but it damaged me in some ways. I was left feeling that I was never good enough, and that no matter what I did, no matter what I achieved, there would always be some disappointment attached to that. It's so sad to think back on this, especially now that I know that what I was trying to make better, trying to fill up and compensate for, was my mother's lifetime of loss, compromises and sacrifices. The reality was and is that there was really no way for me to make that better. I couldn't erase her pain or memories or heal old wounds for her, much as I wanted to. That time had passed, that door had closed.

And then there was the unspoken trauma and grief of having to leave their homeland, friends, community and home for a new country. To this day, nearly fifty years later, my mother still tells me how she doesn't feel like Australia is truly home. That's sad enough, but to make matters worse she's really caught between two lands. She has been away from Greece so long that she is no longer seen as Greek there, but of course in Australia that's just what she is seen as. She has spent most of her lifetime, emotionally, waiting for true acceptance.

Mum has been back to Greece three times but the last visit in 2000 when my Dad died was so traumatic she hasn't been back since. I hope to persuade her to travel with me to Greece next year, so we can make some happy memories for her to keep when she comes home.

Moving to a new country, learning a new language and new rules meant more struggle and sacrifice for both my parents. Where could my mum and dad's grief go? Who ever saw it, recognised it or acknowledged it? The truth is no one did. How do you heal when you have children to raise in a foreign land and you are in survival mode every hour of every day without any rest from it? Who grieves for you?

And yet my cherished values of integrity, humility, compassion, empathy, kindness, resilience and caring about my community all come from my dad and mum. They showed me these values in action through their sacrifices and their selflessness. All the best parts of me

My parents sitting on my dad's car in Mount Beauty.
My mother is wearing her favourite dress.

come from them and I'm so grateful. For all the heartache and chaos in the family home growing up and all the hurt I carried from it, I also carry the profound love that they gave me. That is the love of putting themselves last every time so Nola and I could be first, every time.

My sister has always been my best friend. Nola is two years younger than me but we were joined at the hip from the youngest age. We've always been similar in so many ways. We both had little confidence or self-esteem and were awkward growing up, but we had so much resilience. And naturally, we share the same values and the same passions.

Nola's always had the biggest heart and mind. We know each other's pain so well, having watched each other survive it each day from an early age. We were so simpatico that we didn't need to do more than look at one another to know that as long as we had each other we could get through whatever was thrown at us. And despite some very rocky moments, that's been pretty much how things have played out. We have absolute total trust in each other, and even when we argue or fight, it's only minutes (or maybe a couple of hours!) until we move on.

My sister is also a brilliant, multi-award-winning criminal and human rights barrister. She was my first legal volunteer, ready to help at the ASRC from the day it opened. I remember during her first couple of years as a barrister, still in her late twenties, Nola was routinely in the Federal Court, fighting to protect refugees. Despite often being up against Senior Counsels and QCs twice her age, she fought for each refugee fearlessly and fiercely – simply incredible.

She is so very special in my life. I honestly could not have made it without her. I love no one more than my sister. Nola elevates me every day by being the human being, friend, sister and role model she is for me. I don't know how the universe decided to bless me with my own guardian angel, but it did in her.

2

CHILDHOOD

I was born in Albury in country New South Wales, but I have always felt that I was Greek, that I was from somewhere else. I looked different from all the other kids. They had names like Smith and Jones and I was Karapanagiotidis. Having such a handle, I guess it's no surprise they used to call me Mr Alphabet, which at least was more imaginative than 'dirty wog'. But no matter what I was called, it was hard to ignore the fact that I didn't fit in.

Our first home was in Mount Beauty, a small country Victorian town around 350 kilometres from Melbourne, nestled in the Kiewa Valley and with a population of around one thousand. It remains a haven for skiers in winter with Falls Creek just thirty minutes away, and in summer it's a great place for tourists looking for a laid-back family holiday with no complications. The town is surrounded by epic mountains, their snow-capped peaks visible throughout the winter months. And nearby is the Kiewa River and waterways I spent most of my childhood neck deep in. It all sounds idyllic, I know, but it was far from that for a young wog like me in country Victoria in 1970s Australia.

I vividly remember our yellow weatherboard home that looked just a little tired, its flaky, peeling paint the result of countless hot country summers. Inside, nearly every surface was covered in different types of plastic, from the lino floors to the laminex bench tops, cupboards and bathroom cabinets, to vinyl nearly everywhere else. The furniture in the house very loudly echoed the early 1970s, including leopard-patterned dressers that would now be treasured in the homes of hipsters. And with a typically migrant touch, doilies covered all the remaining bare surfaces. Our wooden framed 1970s Panasonic TV, which only had two channels, often blared in the background.

A familiar memory from around this time – I was around eight and Nola about six – was me trying to put together some sort of evening meal for us. More often than not, Mum and Dad would work an extra shift on the tobacco farm and not come home until after 10 pm. I wasn't the most expert of cooks back then, and I remember eggs burning, baked beans spilling out of the can and onto the table, missing the plate entirely, and my sausages looking as if they'd been cooking for over a week, more cinders than anything else. I can still recall that smell went through the entire house. And all the while Nola, with her pigtails and rosy cheeks, was looking up at me, all curious, her brow slightly furrowed.

My sister and I grew up sharing a bedroom where, to her great dismay, I would practise moves memorised from an obsessive attention to the weekend television's World Wrestling Federation, where Hulk Hogan was king.

I also had a cat, a ginger cat, named Ginger, of course. Most days it would hide underneath the house and wait for my dad to come home, because he was the only person in the family who was always gentle with him. In fact, I shamefully remember terrorising him as a child by trying to stuff him in the letterbox. To what purpose I simply can't recall.

The truth is that I really have only one enduring happy memory of my childhood in Mount Beauty and it has everything to do with my father. Nola and I didn't see that much of our parents around this time. They would be both up and gone early each morning and off to work in the fields picking tobacco, often not coming home until after we had put ourselves to bed. But each and every night when Dad came home – and it didn't matter how long he had been out there in the dirt and the dust, how late he had been working – he always remembered to bring home a chocolate bar for me. It was usually a Scorched Peanut

Bar. This ritual was my father's way of showing his love for me. Of course he carried his love on his back in those soul-destroying tobacco fields, which was gift enough, but he also handed it to me as a treat at the end of each day to show how much he cared.

Home was such a complex place growing up. So many nights, even very late, I was called on to mediate an argument between my parents, even as a young boy. Now that I'm much older I understand that I was growing up in a deeply traumatised home. My parents were carrying the trauma experienced by their own parents who had survived two world wars, and, in my father's case, an extended period of ethnic cleansing that forced his parents to begin their adult lives as refugees. They all grew up in brutal, unforgiving poverty and hardship. As mentioned, my mother and father weren't allowed to complete primary school and learn better skills, thus suffering all the loss that decision brought about, and both had strict, austere fathers who never expressed their emotions – but then, of course, there is no time for such indulgences when you're busy just trying to survive.

It became apparent pretty early on that it was up to me to be the emotional adult in the home. I became the mediator between my parents as they argued about how the other had let them down. I would listen to the grievances of each of them – all their hurt, pain and

My father loved posing for photographs, any time and anywhere. Here he is in Mount Beauty in the summer of 1974.

disappointment for their lives never lived – soaking it in like a sponge. It was agonising. Unsurprisingly, I had no answers. But even more painful was that I had no way to take their hurt and grief away.

I felt like I had to take a side, to be the umpire for who had been more wounded, who was sacrificing more than the other, who was working harder, caring more and being the better parent to my sister and me. This ended up making me feel that love was always conditional, in spite of knowing that my parents loved me no matter what and had sacrificed everything for us. It was a source of great confusion and pain for me. And this was only further reinforced because whose side I took determined whose love I would receive that day.

So the ongoing lesson I learned from this, as touched on earlier, was that I always felt like a disappointment to my parents – or at least one of them at any given time. No matter how much I achieved or how hard I worked, it was never enough. There would always be recriminations and a suffocating unhappiness. There would always be something else to criticise, or fret about or be disappointed in.

My father numbed himself with alcohol and Valium; and my mum was consumed by a grief and sadness that at times threatened to consume her. But always they both just did their best to stay afloat. My father was like so many migrants at that time, failed also by the largely racist, indifferent health system. Instead of having a doctor who listened to him and made some effort to get him some help with mental health, the GP put my father on a lifetime of Valium to numb the pain he never escaped.

Once I was a little older and we had moved to Melbourne, I remember sitting on the verandah with Dad, trying so hard to connect with him. My dad often felt that we were all against him, that we ganged up on him as a family, given that Mum was never satisfied because of her own grief too. I would try my best to listen and understand, but it would always end in despair for all of us. And in those times I tried to stand up for my mum emotionally, my dad would feel like I had betrayed him. I could see that he just felt so alone, while I just felt so angry. There was the angry thirteen-year-old me, the angry twenty-year-old me and then there was the twenty-seven-year-old me who no longer had a dad. So quickly all of that anger, years of it, turned to a poisonous grief. To this day I wish I could go back and tell my father he was always enough for me, that I was proud of him and needed him.

So while it wasn't always effective and it took a bit of time, at a young age I had to find a way to hold my shit together emotionally, so that when things were falling apart around me, I wasn't. I think from those evenings I learned that my real role was to be there to care for others, to be the one who makes everything okay. The person who pushes through no matter how much they would rather hide or run away.

So while all of this slowly made me more resilient, it also made me more disconnected from myself, and, together with this immense pressure to always do the right thing, the responsible thing, I lost something in me. I lost the right to ask for help, to be vulnerable and not to always be in control of my surroundings and, most importantly, my emotions. Instead I felt guilty for everything. I felt that my emotional needs didn't matter and that I had to be stoic and strong at all times. I didn't know how to be emotionally present with anyone; I was never taught how to be.

I honestly had no idea how to show my feelings. Until my early twenties I didn't even know how to hug someone properly or give someone a kiss on the cheek without getting anxious. My dad would show me his love with a gentle punch on the shoulder, though once I had reached adolescence I don't remember my mum ever hugging me. But then no one had held them or given them this kind of affection. It wasn't their fault.

Looking back, I can see that my mum and dad were brought together as much by necessity as love, and they had to endure adversity together on a daily basis. There was precious little time for romance or date nights; they had a family to start, raise and support.

IT'S NEVER
TOO LATE
FOR HEALING
TO HAPPEN.

So it's a special joy now to watch my mum in her new role as a grandmother and to see the nurturing, love, affection and attention she gives to my little nephew, Leo. I watch her healing each day in his presence and it's so beautiful. My mum and I hug now, too. At first I'd found it difficult because it brought back this hurt, but now I really treasure it: to hold my mum and let her know I love her and to let her show her unfailing love for me. So it turns out it's never too late for healing to happen.

3

SCHOOL

I used to be jealous of the Anglo-Australian boys. They were popular, they were athletes, and they were hairless. I envied them being so 'normal' when I could scarcely be further from it. At the age of ten I was sprouting the signs of my first moustache, and I had dark, hairy arms and legs. No girl would look at me, ever. And yet I also remember being rebellious and refusing to fit in. I have faint memories from the days of prep of fighting back when kids tried to bully me in the playground.

And I remember a really confronting incident that occurred in Grade 3. The teacher had said to the class, 'Put your hand up if you're Australian.'

My hands stayed still, resting anxiously by my sides, the only ones in the room not in the air.

She looked at me slightly baffled. 'You're Australian, Kon. You're one of us.'

At the age of seven, already fiercely defiant, I said red-faced with passion, 'No, I'm not. I'm Greek.'

The teacher gave me a deep look of disappointment and then a thorough dressing down in front of the class. On reflection I suspect she was surprised and then annoyed with me for speaking out – something I still do.

My early school memories are basically a combination of three things that were repeated with mind-numbing frequency: of regularly being told to 'fuck off back to where you came from', being bullied daily for being a wog, and an overwhelming feeling of not fitting in *anywhere*. I remember I used to wish I could just vanish off the face of the earth.

One saving grace was my best childhood friend, Arthur Pavlidis. We were the two little wog boys in the whole town. We stuck together like glue until my moving to Melbourne tore our friendship apart. One of my favourite photos is of the two of us about to walk to school for our first day. I have my brand-new Snoopy bag on my shoulders. We are wearing our best, perfectly ironed shorts and have huge grins on our faces, full of hope and anticipation. Tragically, Arthur died seven years ago. I really miss him.

Something else to be thankful for around this time was that the township of Mount Beauty was mostly kind to my parents. While they certainly didn't embrace my parents, the residents respected how hard they worked and cared

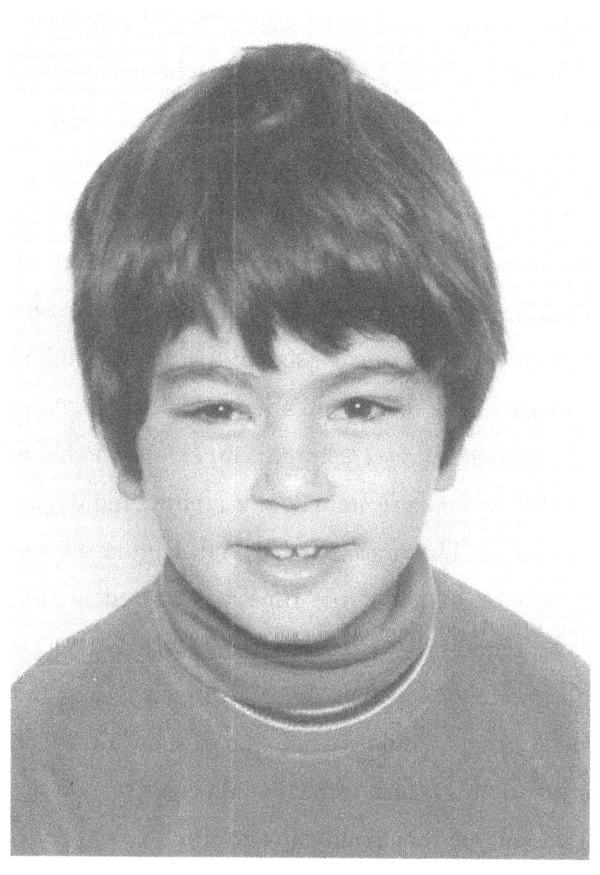

Me at around six years old, in my favourite jumper and one of the turtleneck shirts I loved to wear as a child.

for their kids, and I do look back on this with gratitude. I don't, however, have any such memories for me.

We moved to Melbourne when I was twelve. Just consider for a moment that I was in Year 7 and the month was September. This meant that the school year had only one more term to go, marking it as a disastrous time to join a new high school and try to fit in. But it happened.

After years of broken promises my father had finally agreed to my mum's wish to move to the city. All of our relatives lived there and for her the hope of an easier life beckoned. My parents had assumed that we would both go to a private Greek school and not a public school. Nola and I flatly refused. We were utterly inflexible on this point. We both felt that a private school was elitist and we wanted no part of it. That meant that I ended up at Thornbury High School, which at the time was ranked in the Top 10 worst schools in Victoria by the *Herald Sun* (seriously). I still remember my first day and my first class and the teacher asking, 'Would anyone like to show Kon around?' That question was met with stony silence.

I was on my own from day one.

So my dreams that living in the city and going to a multicultural school where kids like me were in the majority would mean an end to being bullied and not fitting in were quickly quashed. Kids just found new words, reasons and ways to hate and bully me.

Looking back now, I can also see other reasons I was such an easy target. I would admit to doing my homework, I wasn't tough or aggressive, and I didn't know how to handle myself around girls. What was probably worse was that I didn't dumb myself down.

Thank God for books. I enjoyed reading and I wanted to do well at school, so I turned to books for succour and solace. I would hide in the library at lunchtimes to avoid walking around the school where no one would look at me, talk to me or smile at me. I would hide there so people couldn't see just how alone and unwanted I was in this world. And I would also hide there to stop being bullied. But while I was there I would escape into other worlds. Most of my time in the library was spent reading to find some answers about my place in the world.

And after school was done for the day, I would go home and cry on my bed for a while. This became my daily ritual.

I felt so lost and confused about why I couldn't fit in and why I couldn't make sense of things. I kept asking myself so many questions: Why are you making it so hard for yourself? Why don't you know when to shut up? Why don't you smile at the stupid things these bullies say and mock the strange kids that don't fit in, so you can? But I couldn't do that because I kept looking at these kids and thinking that those kids are me. At the time I think I disappeared into myself a great deal. Sure, I was a teenage boy, and I know those years are often hard for many people, but when I came home from school I would say to the mirror, 'You are a worthless piece of shit.' Every. Single. Day.

I hated myself. God, how I hated myself. I couldn't even imagine that I might ever experience love from another person. And yet, even during all of this pain and self-loathing, I think I came to an implicit understanding that life was about more than just me.

Through my reading I became interested in history, and especially the civil rights movement in the United States. And during those lunchtimes in the library I came across a book by the Reverend Martin Luther King, Jr called *Strength to Love.* There I was, a fourteen-year-old kid going to one of the crappiest public schools in Melbourne, coming from a racist little country town, and I came across a book that didn't just change my life but *saved* my life.

Martin Luther King was such an extraordinary man who, against the odds, used to speak about leading with love. This man wrote about how the greatest and most beautiful thing you can do is honour your integrity, honour your inner voice and spirit. 'The ultimate measure of a man is not where he stands in moments of comfort and convenience, but where he stands at times of challenge and controversy.' Those words by Martin Luther King just poured out of the book straight into my heart.

King wrote about how the most important thing you can do is never compromise who you are. And instead of your uniqueness, your identity being a fragile and shameful thing, it's an extraordinary unspoken thing of beauty, of power, of possibility. In this book, a man was writing just to me, and telling me that caring about the world, aching for the world even at this tender age, was a thing to be proud of. 'Along the way of life, someone must have sense enough and morality enough to cut off the chain of hate. This can only be done by projecting the ethic of love to the center of our lives.'

Strength to Love taught me many lessons as a teenager – it helped provide clarity and it gave me some self-acceptance. It also hinted at what my vocation would be. I had no peer group growing up as a teenager, and because of that I had learned to become pretty solitary, to become self-sufficient. This self-sufficiency I would later learn was both a gift and a hindrance to the adult me, and self-sufficiency isn't necessarily self-acceptance. *Strength to Love* taught me that being vulnerable and real matters, even if no one else sees it. It was all about authenticity and integrity, about values, and about love – including self-love in order to help give love. 'Love is the most durable power in the world,' King wrote.

I went back to that book throughout my teenage years for comfort whenever I wavered and thought that if I just did what everybody expected from me then my pain would stop. That if I gave up my idealism I would finally belong. But Martin Luther King's words didn't stop reverberating for me back then. On the contrary, they've continued to be hugely important throughout my life and I'll draw on them again through these pages. That's not to say, though, that I have always lived by them. We are all works in progress and sometimes our progress stalls – that too is a part of life.

Most teenagers are sensitive to everything around them and I was no different. I saw injustice everywhere I looked, and I felt it in my own little world each day.

When I was fifteen I remember my Maths teacher telling me to drop out of school because I would never amount to anything and that I should just stop wasting her time. How can a teacher be allowed to speak to a student like this? Surely she had responsibilities and a duty of care? It seems outrageous that she could have spoken to a student in such a way. Thank God I really did want to do well at school, because I didn't listen to her. And I would hate to think how much damage she might have inflicted on a less stubborn and pig-headed soul than me.

One night, at the age of sixteen, I was in my pyjamas, standing on the road outside my home. It was late, close to midnight, and I was standing in front of our 1969 white Valiant. My dad had just threatened to walk out on us. I was begging him not to. My hands were flat on the car's bonnet and I had convinced myself that as long as I was blocking the car with my body he couldn't go anywhere. A year earlier it had been Mum threatening to leave, and back then, again, I was the one to restore the peace. Each time they both relented. Each time it caused me a great deal of distress – grief and anger at how life for them had been so cruel and unfair. And seeing my parents' relationship so frequently break down like this made it difficult for me to even fathom how people could live together harmoniously.

Then at the age of eighteen I came to a real crossroads. I remember staring into the mirror with such a deep sense of disgust and shame. Up to this point I had felt disconnected from everyone and feared any form of physical intimacy. In fact, I couldn't even imagine having a real friendship, so the prospect of a relationship was more than impossible.

So there I was staring in the mirror.

Kon, how could anyone ever love this? I thought to myself. *How could you ever be loved?*

I wanted the earth to swallow me up, right then and there, so I didn't have to suffer any more. And then I realised that I had a choice: I was either going to end it all and find a way to take my own life or I was going to find a way to fight through this. And I knew that bottled up deep, deep inside me there was all this love that was just waiting,

SO MAYBE I COULD TAKE ALL THAT HURT AND ANGER AND HATRED THAT WAS CONSUMING ME AND DO SOMETHING BEAUTIFUL WITH IT.

waiting to come out. And yet I remember thinking that I couldn't give it to myself, none of it. This love that was deep inside me, hidden from the world, was waiting to be given to someone, somewhere.

I started to tease this thought out a little more and rationalised it to myself, thinking that if the world doesn't want to love me, then maybe I can still give love back to it. My thinking was that this would then mean love would meet me halfway. In doing so maybe I could feel love, *be* love.

Martin Luther King's words also helped give me greater clarity: 'As my sufferings mounted I soon realised that there were two ways in which I could respond to my situation – either to react with bitterness or seek to transform the suffering into a creative force.'

So maybe I could take all that hurt and anger and hatred that was consuming me and do something beautiful with it. Maybe I could lead with love. And maybe all that ugliness that I felt about myself was in fact not ugliness but transformative, powerful, magical, and that it was all still me. So if I chose love and could love others, then one day I might even be worthy of experiencing love myself.

I think we often have to hit rock bottom before we're willing to hear our own voice. And no other person's voice can transform us into who we are really meant to be. I think it's often in moments of desperation that the greatest chance to grow shows itself. And I think we often miss this moment and retreat back into old habits when instead we need to let go and 'fail forward' – to see the opportunity of failure to reflect, learn and grow – so at least there's *some* progress.

So in that moment I decided I was going to be all the things I wished I could be for myself – kind, loving, compassionate, accepting – for others.

This decision changed my life in ways I could never have imagined. Over the next decade I would take all that love and reach out to any part of our community I saw a bit of myself in – people whom society had turned its back on, had deemed not worthy of welcome, of safety, love or dignity. They were my people, I thought. Maybe I could finally make sense somewhere.

This decision saved my life. When we're filled with self-loathing and have become an island cut off from intimacy, connection and belonging, finding our way back is never easy. The reality is we often double down on it; we carry with us this constant feeling of being an impostor, of being undeserving of belonging.

I can see now that this was an unusual path to self-love and meaning, but surely the most important thing here is that we need to *own* the challenge of finding self-love and meaning in life, otherwise it never comes to us. My reckoning is that if we don't allow people to get close to us, to see us as we are because we have already rejected ourselves, then self-love cannot come. And I don't think there is any right or wrong way to start this healing for any of us. But I do know that leading with empathy, compassion, humility, decency and love gives you a fighting chance to heal yourself.

So in a moment I had made the decision to go out there and give that love to whoever needed it. I believed in that moment. And I thought that in a work environment I could at least leave the world a little kinder and fairer than I had so far found it. So that was what I allowed myself to do.

4

THINGS START TO SHIFT

'You look like you could do with a friend. Do you need a dollar, mate?'

A man who looked to be in his sixties, with little more than the clothes on his back, went to dig into his pre-loved jacket pocket for some coins.

'That's okay, mate,' I said. 'I'm actually one of the volunteers here. My name's Kon.'

I held out my hand to shake his.

'Good to meet you, Kon. I'm George. I remember when I was your age,' he said with a sad smile. 'I remember my family and I miss them so much. None of them will talk to me any more, so I only have memories of them now.'

In 1990 I was sitting breaking bread with two hundred homeless men in Carlton. The day before I had been at university where I was studying Behavioural Sciences, the first of six degrees I would eventually complete. No one there looked at me once. If I died tomorrow, I had thought, no one would notice, no one would even care. Uni was a place of such privilege but it didn't have any of the kindness this homeless man with nothing to his name gave me at that moment – me, a total stranger.

And at that moment I learned one of my most enduring life lessons – that what's most important is how people treat you. What's not important is what they have, who they claim to be, their status, wealth or education. If God is in the details then so is our humanity, and it's found in the small acts of kindness and decency that cost us nothing but give us everything.

Back then I was an awkward eighteen-year-old in search of meaning, looking for a place for my love, a place where I made sense. These men had taken me to their bosom, like a son they hadn't seen in decades. And they *saw* me.

The Hanover Drop-in Centre in Queensberry Street was a vast open space with little to make it feel warm or like home. There were no flowers or plants, no art on the walls, no rugs, and the overhead fluoros flickered incessantly. Its saving graces were a well-worn pool table and a free hot meal, which was provided to all who turned up each day at 12.30 pm. The staff expected me to join them upstairs at lunchtimes. They never ate with the men, which I had

IF GOD IS IN THE DETAILS THEN SO IS OUR HUMANITY, AND IT'S FOUND IN THE SMALL ACTS OF KINDNESS AND DECENCY THAT COST US NOTHING BUT GIVE US EVERYTHING.

thought was very strange. In fact, they seemed confused when I insisted that I do just that. My principal role there was to welcome the men and be ready for conversation and friendship, and while I may have been only eighteen, I knew that to build trust and respect with a group of people you have to take the time to sit and share a meal with them. And I knew it meant a lot to the men that I stayed with them at the long tables to eat rather than head upstairs behind closed doors.

Volunteering at the Hanover Centre was a turning point for me in so many ways. Many of these men were my father's or my grandfather's age and I remember thinking how easily it could have been either of them sitting across the table from me. They weren't bad men, though all of them were in some kind of crisis. What had made so many of them homeless was just a moment in time when something had happened that they hadn't been prepared for: losing their job when they were living week to week to cover the rent or mortgage; the sudden end of a marriage; the death of a partner or parent; or remembering childhood sexual abuse, or experiencing it as an adult male. There are so many ways our lives can quickly spiral out of control if a support structure suddenly disappears. Take a moment to reflect on how fragile your own security might be. Imagine if those closest to you were suddenly taken, or you lost your job and had no one to take care of you. How would you cope?

It might sound strange but I felt so extraordinarily lucky to have found that place, because I truly was useful there. My empathy, humility and perspective helped me create a safe space where the men felt heard and supported. All the things that had traumatised me as a kid and had left me with shame and guilt were at last the very things that connected me with those men and made me feel like a kindred spirit. I was able to draw on all that love I had in me and show these men the compassion, kindness and warmth I wished I could have had for myself.

Over the next ten years I went on to spend around forty hours over seven days a week as a volunteer for twenty-two charities while still studying at university. Society had turned its back on most of the communities I volunteered for – all of them were marginalised, and all of them were places where I made sense and helped make a real difference.

I worked as a volunteer at the Royal Children's Hospital; and in psychiatric hospitals as a community visitor, a mental health support worker, and a mental health paralegal representing people involuntarily hospitalised. I was a telephone crisis counsellor; an activist campaigning against men's violence to women; a youth outreach worker; a tenancy advice worker; a sexual assault counsellor; an advocate, researcher and legal adviser to people living with HIV and AIDS; an outreach worker supporting women working as sex workers; a community educator; a soup kitchen cook; and a campaigner to stop women who were coming out of prison from dying.

I seized every opportunity I could to connect, contribute and be a part of something that mattered. I wanted my life to have real meaning and purpose. I wanted to honour the sacrifices my parents made for me and to feel like I was making the world a little kinder and fairer. This intensive busyness was one of the most incredible privileges of my life. I received so much more than I ever gave – you always do when you volunteer. People would entrust me with their most intimate stories, speak of their dreams and desires and show me their deepest scars. How precious it is for people to share themselves like this. How lucky I was that these people trusted me enough to ask for help.

As chance would have it, when the Social Work course I was doing at the time temporarily lost its accreditation in 1994, I decided to drop it for a while, and I distinctly recall a fellow student saying to me, 'Beggars can't be choosers.'

I didn't miss a beat. 'I'm no beggar,' I replied. 'One always has choices.' And making the decision to volunteer for as much of that year as I could led me to have the most amazing life-changing experiences.

My Sundays at the Royal Children's Hospital were always both a joy and a heartache. Every second Sunday I would spend the day playing with terminally ill children and supporting their parents as a volunteer for Very Special Kids. I always stood out; at the time the average age of the volunteers was around sixty and there was me just in my twenties, hairy, chunky and filled with passion. I remember so many beautiful children, including Tom, who was wheelchair-bound with severe cerebral palsy. The simple act of strolling around the hospital grounds where the sun could kiss him whole gave him so much pleasure. And I remember five-year-old John, whose morning 'I made' after a fierce and robust game of hide-and-seek in the hospital.

The flipside to all of this volunteering, though, was how affected I was by the injustice of it all. For so many of the marginalised there were these recurring themes of unresolved trauma, grief and loss. Cruelty can be so costly, and I would often think 'if only' – if only they had access to counselling to deal better with their first crisis: if only they had that rehab bed when they first sought help for their addiction, or a spare bed at a woman's refuge to escape an abusive husband, or timely access to public housing.

In all the years I've been doing this, I still can't bear such inequality and I will never be a bystander to such injustice. I will not accept a country that leaves anyone behind; that's not my country. Every day I'm criticised for helping refugees because we should be 'helping our own homeless'. Well, they are *all* our own – be they refugees, new migrants, Indigenous people, people with disabilities, at-risk youths, LGBTIQA communities, homeless, the unemployed, or people with drug and alcohol issues. They are all someone's daughter, son, mum, dad, friend, neighbour, but, most importantly, they are *someone*. That's enough.

If everyone who talks about 'helping our own' actually did just that, we wouldn't even have a homelessness problem. As a society we invest so much time and energy into not helping people by raging against people who really do care. What a waste. People need to be valued and helped back on their feet. You can never help by asking people who are barefoot to lift themselves up by their bootstraps. And contrary to politicians' lazy clichés describing our marginalised people variously as 'bludgers', 'failures', 'burdens', 'dangers, 'sluts', 'welfare cheats' and 'criminals', I have never found this to be the case.

For more than three years I walked the streets of St Kilda every Saturday night until 3 am as an outreach worker for the Prostitutes Collective of Victoria (PCV). All the women I came across were brave and resilient, risking their safety to put food on the table for their families and to keep a roof over their heads. The PCV no longer exists as an organisation, and this was at a time when St Kilda was becoming increasingly gentrified. These new residents' attitudes and their disapproval of sex work pushed these women from the well-lit Fitzroy and Grey streets into darker and darker corners of the suburb. And as the women moved to more isolated public spaces to work, the likelihood of any violence being inflicted – such as theft, assault or rape – also increased.

One of my tasks was to warn sex workers about this by handing out weekly 'Ugly Mug' newsletters, effectively mugshots of men who we knew had been violent to women. I was also there to provide them with condoms, information and referrals for help if they wanted them, and the women were always so grateful for the support.

The potential clients, in contrast, drove around, hooning, in packs. They spat at the women, verbally abused them and threw eggs and water balloons at them to humiliate them. And yet I only ever saw the police arresting, warning or giving a hard time to the women. Not once did I see them taking issue with the men. We criminalise women's bodies while allowing men to do as they wish. I am so sick of men who slut-shame women who are sex workers. The women I have known who had this job have always been smart, kind, strong, compassionate people. When we strip people of their agency and humanity, we send a message that their right to be safe, to live free of violence, to be treated with respect and have human rights are all conditional. Me? I see only people. Human beings. And this echoes yet another memorable

Martin Luther King quote: 'Too seldom do we see people in their true *humanness*.'

Around this time, too, I was doing some volunteer work for male survivors of sexual abuse. I had got to know a number of people from other charities and one day I got a call from Sister Bernadette who was working for the Australian Red Cross. She asked me if I might give free trauma counselling to a few young refugees who had been tortured. Of course I was happy to do so, and the first man she sent was from Turkey. Mehmet was about the same age as me and he had been tortured by his country's government. I became his trauma counsellor, and through our sessions together over a number of months he began to heal from the torture he had experienced. Then I was sent a few more refugees to counsel. And that's when things really started to move.

5

A Movement Begins

Today the Asylum Seeker Resource Centre is the largest organisation helping people seeking asylum in Australia. Since it opened its doors in 2001, more than fifteen thousand people have helped save thousands of lives, and all without a single dollar of federal government funding. We're now based in a building directly across the road from where it all began. The centre now, though, is up to one hundred and fifty times bigger, with thirty-six life-changing programs available to provide assistance with food, legal support, advocacy, aid, employment, education, health, mental health and community development. And there is a team of 175 paid staff and over 1,300 volunteers helping more than 5,000 people seeking asylum from sixty countries.

Its beginnings, however, were far more humble.

The ASRC started as a TAFE class project for a group of students I was teaching to be welfare workers. The subject

Welfare Studies students from Victoria University TAFE sorting out donations before the ASRC's official opening.

was called Community Work and it required the students to spend a number of weeks in a community placement. They each had to decide which not-for-profit they wanted to spend six weeks with, but in class the following week they all came back to tell me they couldn't find any charity that would take them for just that limited period of time. What else could we do?

I wanted my students to know that they were powerful and could make a difference, and that they didn't need a piece of paper to be able to do so. They were an amazing mix of people who had already worked so hard just to be in that classroom with me. They included incredible single mums like Nancy, mothers returning to study twenty years after raising a family like Penny, and newly arrived migrants and refugees like Waly. I wanted them all to know that if they led with their hearts, imaginations and potential, they could create anything.

I thought for a moment then looked at them with the beginnings of a smile. 'Well,' I said, 'how about we start our own charity as our class project?'

I knew that many people seeking asylum in Melbourne on bridging visas had nowhere to turn for food and that many were going hungry. At first they thought I was joking, but once I persuaded them I was deadly serious, credit to them, they all said yes on the spot. The next thing to decide was what to call our organisation. We knew we would be helping asylum seekers by providing food and so we quickly settled on the Asylum Seeker Resource Centre.

We started in a tiny shopfront of twenty square metres in the working-class city suburb of Footscray. The space was provided rent-free by my incredible friend Pablo Gimenez, who was running a not-for-profit organic grocery store next door. It was Pablo who made it all possible.

After securing our HQ, I broke the students up into four working groups: one painted our little office with the brightest yellow paint I could find; another approached local supermarkets and food markets for food donations; the third organised the opening-day street party and contacted media; and the final group built the shelves that would hold our food donations.

The furniture was donated by my mum – a small table from her kitchen was repurposed as the reception desk, and the new shelves against the bright happy walls helped create a warm, cosy place of welcome. There were rows of tinned beans, and packets of rice, flour and sugar. Pablo pitched in further and gave us some fresh fruit and vegetables from his shop next door, and that was it.

On 8 June 2001, eight weeks from that first conversation with my students, founded on little more than the power of hope, the ASRC opened its doors.

We started with this modest food bank, which we opened two days a week, scraping together whatever food we could source. We got by with just enough food for a couple of hours each day, and always, always some small miracle would happen to stretch things. A box of rice, or flour, or tuna or honey would simply appear, or a kind stranger would drop in and hand us twenty or fifty dollars and we would rush to the markets to get whatever people needed most. Weekends were spent with Mum driving me around trying to make that one hundred or two hundred dollars from donations go as far as it could – Not Quite Right grocery clearance stores were always my first port of call – and then I dug into my own pocket to make up the difference.

Incidentally, I lost my teaching job for starting the ASRC as a class project. The university thought that what I had done was too political and that I had jeopardised its relationship with the federal government. And it's true that at that time standing up for people seeking asylum was seen as high-risk, so few major institutions wanted to take a moral stance. But if I hadn't been sacked it's more than likely that the ASRC wouldn't be here today.

And then in late August 2001, just a few months after we opened our doors, there was the *Tampa* crisis. For those of you too young to remember this clearly, 438 people, mostly Afghan asylum seekers, were rescued from a failing Indonesian fishing boat by Norwegian cargo ship the MV *Tampa* around 140 kilometres north-west of

Christmas Island. The *Tampa*'s captain had declared a state of emergency and entered our waters against Australian authorities' instructions. The ship anchored near Christmas Island, where SAS troops boarded, and so began a five-day stand-off between the Norwegian captain and the Howard government over where these refugees should be taken. The federal government scrambled to table its new Border Protection Bill, which although defeated in the Senate, established the so-called Pacific Solution. This policy determined that all asylum claims would be processed offshore, and it helped serve as the architecture for the hellholes that would rise up on Manus Island and Nauru.

'We will decide who comes to this country and the circumstances in which they come,' Howard had proclaimed at the time, using language that set aflame a bigoted nationalistic view that our borders were suddenly under threat. And then, after 9/11 a few weeks later, Howard added further fuel to the fire by implying there would be a higher risk of future terrorist acts if Australia was not tough now on protecting its borders and turning back this boatload of people seeking asylum. Such words preyed on people's fears and anxiety of the unknown – those faceless, desperate souls who had washed up on our shores. And John Howard rode our fear and ignorance all the way to another convincing election win, while refugees have been paying the price ever since.

The official opening day of the ASRC, 8 June 2001, with some of the students who helped make it all possible.

Every day we opened, we worried how we were going to stock the shelves, but as the *Tampa* crisis unfolded we started to get a stream of concerned citizens coming in and saying things like 'I can't keep screaming at the TV, here's fifty dollars', or 'I can't stand feeling so ashamed of my government so here's a box of tinned tomatoes', or 'I don't want to feel so helpless, how can I help?' The *Tampa* crisis made people aware of this terrible issue and many became energised by it.

The ASRC's hand-to-mouth predicament was partly because of a central principle that continues to this day – *not* to accept any federal government funding. I felt then, and still do, that it's better to go down standing on your own two feet than to live on your knees. I had seen way too many charities lose their way, lose their voice and lose their power, compromised and no longer able to tackle or hold to account the authorities responsible for the misery of the people they sought to assist. I did not want us to be a bandaid organisation. I had promised myself that we would be the opposite of everything I had seen as a volunteer that smacked of compromising one's values and integrity just to keep your funding. We would be fearless, holistic and turn no one in need away.

As a result of relying solely on the goodwill of the community, we were on the brink of closing our doors at the end of every month for at least the first five years.

But without fail, just as we really started to worry about what was going to happen, out of nowhere a carload of food would arrive, either from a school food drive or from a local business wanting to do their bit. Or maybe a cheque came in the mail from an anonymous donor telling us it was their way of not feeling helpless or of dealing with their shame at our government's treatment of refugees.

I remember one month being down to our last few thousand dollars and knowing we had just two weeks before we would have to shut up shop. So I went out and begged for money. I didn't sugarcoat anything. I told people how desperate the situation was and people responded, people gave. It was a lesson I never forgot: do not be afraid to ask for help and know that most people want to help, they are just often not asked to. Another time in an effort to keep our doors open, Nola, myself and two volunteers cooked dinner for well over five hundred people to raise funds. I remember sleeping four hours over three days to make that meal possible, but we did whatever was needed to keep our doors open.

And that's pretty much how it's been from time to time ever since.

Some months after we opened, and after *Tampa* helped ignite the public, the space upstairs next door became available for one hundred dollars a week. I jumped at the opportunity for the ASRC to expand, and it felt like a

DO NOT BE AFRAID TO ASK FOR HELP AND KNOW THAT MOST PEOPLE WANT TO HELP.

luxury to have more space to help refugees. We had one phone line, staffed by Joan Lynn, a volunteer who still answers our phones on Mondays and Thursdays, and we had one computer, which had a virus, and no working printer. Every time we needed to print something we would cross the road to the office of our local MP, Nicola Roxon, and ask her staff if they could print whatever it was for us. And they did.

Soon after this move, a diminutive, elderly woman from Timor-Leste asked me if we would give English lessons and, on cue, just days later three wise and wonderful women – Toni, Dorothy and Marianne – offered to run ESL classes. A week later the classes began. It was that simple: we saw a need and we did something about it, with no excuses.

Next we had people seeking asylum who needed legal representation to fight for their asylum claim. By this time, I had completed a Law degree and was working as a lawyer so I thought, I can help with that. And so we started our legal service.

Then, increasingly, we started seeing health problems. Mum and dads would turn up to our doorstep daily with their sick, untreated children. 'The hospital turned us away because it wasn't life-threatening,' they would explain. I knew they weren't eligible for Medicare, weren't permitted to work and that most of them had no money. And clearly their children were ill. I remember a weeping father imploring, 'Please help me, my child is sick.' I met women eight months pregnant who had not seen a doctor once since conceiving, and I saw children with asthma whose parents couldn't afford a Ventolin inhaler.

Bugger this, I thought to myself. Enough is enough.

I took a Social Work student on placement aside. 'As part of your studies here, I want you to start Victoria's first health service for people seeking asylum.' It began on 8 April 2002.

And this is pretty much what we did and have done ever since. Every time there was a critical need that people seeking asylum alerted us to, we responded. It didn't matter if we lacked the resources or know-how, we learned by doing. The greater risk was in not helping, the greater risk was someone dying or being sent back to their home country to be tortured.

Fast forward to today and the minute you step into the ASRC, you know you are home. It starts with the beaming faces of our reception volunteers and the deep-purple backdrop with its declaration 'Home of Hope'. To the left is our food bank that feeds six hundred families a week and is full of smiling families every day as our volunteers introduce new spices, grains and vegetables to our newest Australians and give advice on how to cook with them.

The smells of hot curries, stir-fries and stews fill the air as lunch is prepared for 250 people. The Mexican oilcloths that cover the community meals tables were all handmade by my mum, another sign of her continued involvement in the ASRC since its beginnings. In the drop-in space children laugh and play while intricate, dense drum rhythms emanate from the music space.

Upstairs, the walls are multicoloured, art fills the walls and greenery is everywhere to make the ASRC feel like somewhere you are welcomed and wanted. At our health service, the ill, traumatised, sick and pregnant are cared for and their dignity is always respected. Further down the corridor, the intake rooms heave with legal volunteers under the supervision of our lawyers, bearing witness to stories of torture, trauma and war in order to document people's refugee claims and to win their freedom. Still further along the corridor, our social workers and counsellors provide comfort and support for these traumatised people.

Moving downstairs, the feeling is a little more buoyant because this is where our Innovation Hub is based. Here refugees are taught English at all levels, young men borrow suits for their first job interview, women gather in the women's-only space to share their dreams of their new small business or social enterprise, and young people hone their public-speaking skills in our leadership programs. The phones run hot with requests for our catering and cleaning services, while our mentors teach job-interview skills. And then cheers erupt for our latest graduates who have just gained their first Australian qualification or first job in Australia.

None of these breathtaking developments could have occurred without the public's ongoing acts of kindness, the tens of thousands of them who have powered the ASRC since it opened in 2001. From its very modest beginnings it has grown to become a thirteen-million-dollar charity. That's the power of *us* when we come together for a common good.

6

JUSTICE AND EQUALITY

If we are going to create the inclusive, just and welcoming country we yearn for then we need to make sure we have solid values to live by. We cannot expect such change to come from our hollow-hearted political leaders; it can only come from us – bottom-up, grassroots change grounded in our shared moral compass.

Whether the issue is male violence against women, homelessness, drug rehabilitation, asylum seekers' rights, greater representation for the LGBTIQA community, or listening to the voices of Indigenous people, Muslim people or people with disabilities, we need to be mindful that these issues *all* matter. These issues are not in conflict with one another. All of them demand that the individuals who comprise these groups be acknowledged, valued and heard, all of them insist that everyone be *seen*. This is about our humanity. As the civil rights activist Audre Lorde once said, 'There is no such thing as a single-issue struggle because we do not live single-issue lives.'

There will be many moments in your life where you will be tested, where it will be a challenge for you to stay true to your values in that moment. Nothing can prepare you for what might happen next. Yet by staying in that moment and following your heart and conscience, I believe you will always be okay and do the right thing.

One Sunday many years ago, I was walking down Fitzroy Street in St Kilda after my shift volunteering for a local charity. Back then especially, it was a street where you weren't surprised if things got ugly – it was just that kind of place. I was on my way home when I saw a guy and two women hassling another woman, and they were just about to hit her. Well, they were actually going to beat the shit out of her. In an instant, before I even had time to think about it, I put myself between them to act like a human shield. There may have been a second where I thought, What the hell am I doing? But things moved pretty quickly after that.

The three assailants spat all over me. They even took turns at it, one after the other. They spat on me with malicious glee, waiting for me to stop protecting the woman. I vividly remember how time slowed, how the incident seemed to last for hours when it must have been only a few minutes. Saliva and phlegm, clear and green, great gobs of it, soaked into my jumper. They really hawked it up to make sure it counted. I didn't, couldn't move. I was disgusted, of course, but I knew that my sodden jumper was a small price to pay if it stopped them from beating up this woman.

The police arrived and I explained what was going on, but all they saw were four poor people with likely drug issues. They hung around waiting for the aggressors to leave but they didn't ask for any of our names. My actions were small but I hope everybody would have done the same in my situation. No one was hurt and all I had to do was to wash my jumper clean. I believe we have a moral duty to act and intervene when we see something unjust.

A few years later, not long after being admitted as a lawyer, I was to have my first ever court appearance – but it was to be before a single judge in the High Court. (For the non-lawyers reading this, let's just say it's a wild and crazy scenario.)

What had happened was that a dozen desperate mums and dads seeking asylum had asked me to represent them at a directions hearing (a court hearing that sets a timetable for how their legal case will proceed) before the High Court. Apparently, before I became involved, a predatory migration agent had taken what little money they had or were able to borrow and had then abandoned them as their day in court approached. These people had no way of even lodging their High Court applications. So with the help of dedicated volunteer Anita Koochew, who had only just started her Law degree, and young refugee Malik Azzam (whom I had helped release from detention and who had become an incredible ASRC volunteer), I prepared all the urgent applications within forty-eight hours to meet the deadline.

The directions hearing was scheduled a few weeks later and I agreed to appear for the dozen families, thinking it would be a straightforward undertaking. On the day in question in May 2002, as I walked up the steps to the High Court, the twelve mums and dads all started showing me letters they had received in the previous couple of days, letters from the Department of Immigration and the three major law firms representing the federal government. My heart sank. Each letter declared an intention to ask the judge to have all their cases struck out.

I was in trouble and I had no idea what to do. What should have been a formality was now anything but, yet I knew I was all that could stop these twelve families from having their cases struck out, which if it was allowed to happen would mean they would have faced deportation within weeks.

I walked into the Melbourne registry offices of the High Court and in that place was a room full of sunken faces. The people looked so lost and the air was thick with despair and anxiety. As much as I might have wanted to, I couldn't just walk by.

'Who else doesn't have a lawyer?' I asked. More than fifteen hands shot up from around the room. 'Well, then,' I said. 'I'm now your lawyer. Just follow me in.'

What the hell have I done? I thought to myself. Suddenly I now had around thirty clients and was stepping into the High Court with no prep and no clue, clutching a flimsy manila folder and a list of case numbers. How the hell had I got into a scene from *The Castle*?

Inside the courtroom a team of expensive barristers and lawyers, their trolleys bursting with case studies, was busily preparing for the other side, and there I stood, not even sure what to call the judge and with no plan.

All of it felt wrong, unfair. It stank. So when it was my turn I used every ten-dollar word I had and all the passion I could muster to speak up about why these refugees' cases should not be struck out. I didn't know which of the High Court Rules had been breached (truth be told I didn't even have a copy of the High Court Rules on me), but I did know that these three big law firms had colluded to serve my clients with so little notice that they had no fighting chance of being ready.

And that's what I argued for close to an hour on my feet before a single judge of the High Court.

I only sat down when I had run out of words.

Of course the judge knew the law back to front and pointedly asked the other lawyers if they had failed to give the applicants the necessary notice of service required. He then proceeded to rip shreds off my opponents as he determined that laws had indeed been broken. I spent the rest of the day getting up again and again each time one of my clients was called. The judge then gave me the choice of proceeding that day or adjourning all my clients' cases for a couple of months. I turned to my clients who sat in one long row and frantically shook my head to dissuade them from proceeding that day. The case was adjourned and all of the refugees were safe from deportation for at least a couple of months.

As we walked back out into the registry room everyone cheered, and there was a broad, fat smile on every face. It felt incredible. I will never forget that day. I was twenty-nine years old and I had learned unequivocally never to be afraid to stand up for what is right, no matter how scared you are. The government and these law firms had cut corners because they thought no one would care about these human beings. That's how injustice becomes endemic – it relies on the apathy and indifference of people *not* to care enough to stand up and be counted. And that's what our government continues to rely on when it comes to its abuse of refugees.

My greatest challenge yet as a human rights lawyer, however, came a few years later when I answered the phone one evening.

Earlier that day I had been to the Maribyrnong Detention Centre and met with Amir, who was incredibly worried about his young daughter. 'Please save my little girl,' he had begged me in tears. 'She is going to die in here. Please don't let her die. I just want her to be safe, they can leave me here.' Of course I assured him I would do everything I could to keep her safe. I spoke with the Department of Immigration manager of the detention centre and pleaded with him to release the little girl immediately. He told me that the family chose to stay in detention and was free to go home at any time. Just for the record, *home* was a country where the father faced likely execution upon his return.

And so that evening when I answered the phone it was Amir, calling to tell me his ten-year-old daughter had attempted suicide.

'She was unconscious when I found her, Kon. She was hanging from the ceiling with a bedsheet around her neck. Please help me.'

It was clear from his shaky voice that he was in shock. She'd been taken to emergency and I told him I'd meet him there. Once I got to the hospital, though, I couldn't get near her – guards were stationed inside and outside her room. Apparently I was the problem and risk to her, not the last four years of mandatory detention that had driven this little girl to her third suicide attempt. If she hadn't been so small and didn't have such small hands, she would have been successful in tying the bedsheet tight enough to have killed herself. Previously she had tried to poison herself by drinking shampoo and had even started eating her own faeces directly from the toilet bowl. If this had happened in any other setting she would have been moved immediately, but not, it transpired, when the Minister for Immigration was the legal guardian.

So I was turned away by the immigration guards at the hospital. I wasn't sure what to do next but I made a late-night phone call to Julian Burnside, whom I'd never spoken to before. He was incredibly helpful with his advice and support, and, indeed, has continued to be a great support to me and the ASRC for many years now.

After she'd been in hospital for about a week, Immigration planned to return the little girl to the detention centre. I let the authorities know in no uncertain terms that if that occurred it would be the front-page news of every paper the following day. Working with my wonderful colleagues in the refugee sector, we were able to find beds in a specialist mental health hospital for the entire family – they were all terribly traumatised and unwell by this stage – and thereafter to have them released into the community. With Nola's help we fought for their asylum claims and eventually they were accepted as refugees. And every Christmas the father rings to thank us. He never forgets – never. They are now Australian citizens and are thriving.

What's critical to note here is that children in detention and children trying to take their lives in detention are *still* happening. Currently there are still more than 150 kids locked up on Nauru, and the ASRC is trying to have all of them brought to Australia, because after nearly five years of being imprisoned in tents and squalor they are trying to kill themselves.

Late-night emergency phone calls happen far more frequently than I might like but they are part of the job. On another occasion not that long ago my phone woke me at 1 am. I answered it in a haze to hear the voice of desperation on the other end.

'If they deport me tonight, Kon, I'm going to cut my throat. I have a piece of glass here, and if they try anything I'm going to kill myself. I'm serious. Please help me.'

It was Serge, a refugee from Russia. I immediately had to de-escalate the situation, keep him safe and stop the deportation. Serge was certain he would be killed if he was returned to his home country. My challenge was how to persuade him not to slash his throat while simultaneously getting the Department of Immigration to agree not to deport him. I lowered my voice and gently assured him it would be okay. We talked a little more about his situation and he refused to give up the piece of glass to the guards until a guarantee was given. I asked him to hand me over to one of the staff and made it very clear to them that there was no doubt he would kill himself if any attempt was made to forcibly move and deport him. They agreed to back down and then I spoke to Serge again, assuring him that he wouldn't be deported that night. He agreed to relinquish the jagged glass and not harm himself. And so a tragedy was averted, at least for that evening.

I suspect most of us haven't yet thought too long and hard on life-and-death moments, but when any of us has to face them – and we all will – I hope that we choose to hold on to hope and stand up for what is just. Sadly, life-and-death moments are a daily part of working with refugees as the stakes are so high. Refugees are fighting for their very survival in a system that is set up to fail them instead of protecting them. It is rare to have a day at the ASRC when an ambulance isn't called. After years of people being left in legal limbo, often without the right to work or receive any money to survive on, all these people have left to protest with is their bodies.

This is why good people must care, this is why it matters when you raise your voice or give your time in support of the humane treatment of refugees.

And still on the subject of a more just and fairer Australia, why is it that our First Nations people are still being denied their rights? It's unconscionable, particularly given that the group with the highest suicide rate of young males anywhere in the *world* right now is our Indigenous people. This heartbreaking reality comes from our continued systematic racism, our appropriation of Aboriginal land, the absence of a treaty, denial of self-determination, over-policing and lack of investment in their communities.

In 2016 I visited a remote Indigenous community in the Northern Territory. I was there as part of my role as a board member of Children's Ground, a ground-breaking Indigenous organisation that seeks to end generational disadvantage for Aboriginal children. An Indigenous elder wept as she told me how the government was trying to force her off her land, land that her people had lived on for thousands of years. The authorities had cut off the water and electricity, and had refused to provide any public transport to access the land.

I remember looking around at the shabby, ruined buildings and wondering how this could be possible in today's Australia.

I had in fact spent the entire week in distress. In Darwin and Alice Springs, everywhere I looked I saw two worlds, one for white people and one for black. And then it struck me how few adult Aboriginal men were to be seen – so many were already dead, or in prison or away on sorry business.

And it may shock and surprise many of you to know, too, that currently we now have more Aboriginal children in state care than we did during the Stolen Generation years. There is little doubt that we are a country that seeks to silence and ignore the voices of three thousand generations, that holds onto the white fantasy of unoccupied lands, of nothing but bush. We are a country largely indifferent to a fourteen-year-old child being fatally, maliciously run over. A country where ten-year-olds are locked up in prisons in conditions that constitute torture and where suicide is the leading cause of death for our Indigenous youth.

And what does it say about us that we refuse to move the date that we celebrate our nation so that Indigenous people can feel included and part of it? When my father died I wanted the earth to swallow me whole. I needed love, understanding and compassion to hear and honour my sorrow. Why can't we give that to Aboriginal people and change the date of Australia Day? Why is it so hard for everyone to understand that we shouldn't celebrate other people's grief and loss? How can you say you love our country if you don't want to celebrate it on a date that includes everyone, so we can all celebrate together? Where is the justice in that?

MORAL LEADERSHIP IS ABOUT DOING WHAT IS RIGHT, NOT WHAT IS EASY.

We are led by men with vacant imaginations, tinpot hearts and destitute spirits. Political leadership and moral leadership are very different things – moral leadership is about doing what is right, not what is easy, politically expedient or appeals to the lowest common denominator. We have the opportunity for the best leadership to be compassionate and inclusive, not just towards refugees but with how we treat Indigenous people, women's rights and the poor. We could be world leaders but instead we're going backwards on all these fronts.

Speaking up for justice does not have to mean grand gestures and actions. It's in the small daily actions we all make that can help Australia become a fairer place for all to live.

7

THE MOVEMENT IN ACTION

The first Asylum Seeker Resource Centre's membership book – we call refugees 'members' at the ASRC – holds the names of the first 7,529 who came to our door seeking sanctuary. I don't want to forget any of them.

These are the people we first assisted in seeking asylum. They are not numbers. They are people who are custodians of the most extraordinary stories of sacrifice and courage; these people split the world in half and crossed its lands and seas for the love of their family and freedom. Each of these people has a story of heroism. They chose to travel over water because it was safer than remaining on the land from which they had to flee. People are choosing life not death when they travel by sea. They are choosing hope. They are choosing to save their families, not to break a law that doesn't even exist. I remember the faces of each and every one of them – all 7,529 and counting.

I remember Barakat, an unaccompanied fifteen-year-old boy who, when I took on his case as his lawyer, was being locked up with adult men. The reasoning for this was based solely on an unreliable bone-size test that determined he was an adult. It took years of fighting in the courts, with Nola's help as his barrister, to free him. They finally conceded he was a child but it took to the very day he turned eighteen for him to see freedom. Who gives that young man back those three years of his adolescence?

I remember sitting and trying to comfort Mustafa, a father whose five daughters and wife had died while travelling by boat to Australia. He was on a temporary protection visa (TPV), a new type of visa the Howard government introduced in October 1999. This meant that while Australia had accepted him as a refugee, he couldn't sponsor the rest of his family safely and so, rather than face an anguished wait in a dangerous country, that could have lasted a decade or more, they died while trying to reunite with him.

The truth is we actually had a spike in deaths at sea after TPVs were brought in in 1999, with the sinking of the SIEV X on 19 October 2001. In this largest maritime disaster in Australian history, 353 people were killed: 146 of them were children and 142 were women, the majority of whom were trying to reunite with their fathers/husbands who couldn't sponsor them on TPVs. And it should come as no surprise that when people are condemned never to see their family members again, they will simply do anything, take any risk, to do just that. And don't for a minute think that TPVs are a thing of the past – Tony Abbott reintroduced them at the end of 2013, and by the end of 2018 close to twenty thousand people will be on these same damn visas.

What could I possibly have said to a father who had his sky and sun taken from him? And yet Mustafa was not bitter or filled with hate for our country. Without question he was a better man than I will ever be.

I remember the man who had suffered third-degree burns to 80 per cent of his body while in detention, and whom the government had planned to leave to rot. I first met Abbas after he had already been locked up for three and a half years. He was at his end point: every time I saw him he spoke of electrocuting or hanging himself. To free him I had to prove to the authorities that he would die in there otherwise. I arranged for five medical specialists to assess him individually and they all agreed with my prognosis. Yet the government still wouldn't budge. I persisted and I forced the government's hand to undertake its own medical report, a report that was then buried. And then, just as we were preparing to argue for this man's freedom in the Federal Court where the cover-up would have been exposed, Abbas was released. He had been locked up for more than five years.

I remember hiding the entire Homeless World Cup soccer team from Zimbabwe at the ASRC so they had a chance to seek asylum. After frying eggs for them at midnight during an impromptu slumber party, I worked on their asylum claims while they slept. Gratifyingly, all were eventually found to be refugees.

I remember spending time with the amazing Amal Basry, a survivor of the SIEV X, who had sought our protection back in 2001. Amal was a fearless advocate for both the human rights of refugees and an end to the visa class that had trapped her in limbo. 'Kon, they punish me for surviving,' she used to tell me. 'They punish me for not drowning at sea.' And Amal went on to make sure *everyone* heard her words and she *never* stopped making sure people saw the human beings behind the numbers, right up until her death from cancer in March 2006.

I remember our detention rights advocate, Pamela Curr, finding the very troubled Cornelia Rau wasting away in Baxter Detention Centre. Her case was just the beginning of a massive travesty of justice, where it was discovered that 224 Australian citizens or permanent residents were being unlawfully held in Australian immigration prisons. Without question, the sheer scale of this outrageous scandal should have brought down a government – but it didn't.

I recall another occasion – one of many – where our human rights lawyers and Nola as barrister rushed to court at 5 pm on a Friday afternoon to get an injunction to ground a plane that was about to deport a refugee back to life-threatening circumstances. I remember another where a woman who had been raped on Nauru and was now pregnant was told she could either have the baby or go back to Africa where she faced the risk of death. She tried to drown herself in the sea, thinking that was the best option she had. Thankfully the ASRC used all of its independence and went public to demand that she be brought here to Australia. We succeeded and she's now safe.

But there's always bad with the good. I also remember the thousands of children who had lost their childhoods while incarcerated in immigration prisons. Children who, having been recently released from detention, would call our staff at the ASRC 'guard', or when asked their name would quote their Boat ID number because that's what they were called when they were imprisoned. That was all they knew.

I remember the lies of the Children Overboard affair, the SIEV X disaster and, over the last fifteen years, the more than 1100 people whose lives could have been saved if we had provided safe passage. I remember the No Advantage Policy that since 2012 has left 24,500 people in limbo and poverty. I remember Shayan Badraie, the little boy who went mute in detention and on whose file then Immigration Minister Philip Ruddock allegedly wrote

'Bucklies', misspelling 'Buckley's' in reference to the child's odds of being released.

I remember the endless paper trail documenting human rights abuses specifically against children in immigration detention that one day will give rise to a national apology. In 2004 there was *A Last Resort?*, in 2014 Gillian Triggs' *The Forgotten Children* and in 2015 the Moss report, more formally titled *Review into Recent Allegations Relating to Conditions and Circumstances at the Regional Processing Centre in Nauru.* Each of these reports was a catalyst for action, from the growth of the ASRC itself to the birth of other organisations such as Rural Australians for Refugees and Mums 4 Refugees. We were and are all part of the same movement. I remember the sit-downs, protests and the many times health professionals and advocates risked arrest and jail time to speak out for refugees. I remember the celebrations when the refugee movement helped bring to an end Nauru, Manus and TPVs (the first time around) and won people seeking asylum the right to work (the first time around), only to see it all rescinded and the previous cruelties reinstated but in a much more pernicious manner.

So it's good also to remember that there have been lasting success stories too, and one of my fondest and more recent memories concerns baby Asha and her time at the Lady Cilento Hospital.

In February 2016 I had been enjoying a birthday lunch in Brisbane for my friend Ellen Roberts from GetUp!. As we were reminiscing about some of the crazy stuff we had done as refugee advocates, her phone rang. Plans were afoot to deport baby Asha and her mum back to Nauru.

Little baby Asha at only twelve months of age had already had enough hardship for an entire lifetime. She was born in Australia after her refugee mum was brought from Nauru due to a high-risk pregnancy. Despite pleas not to return mother and child, soon after Asha's birth they were both back in a filthy tent inside the Nauru immigration prison. One day while the mother was boiling some water, a table collapsed and water accidentally spilled onto Asha. The baby, suffering burns, was again brought back to Australia for treatment. The hospital's doctors had advised that Asha's life would be in danger if she was again returned to Nauru, though it seems that's exactly what had been planned for that Friday night in February.

For the previous nine days the Brisbane community – inspired by the brave doctors, nurses and staff at Lady Cilento who had refused to let Asha be discharged – had kept an unbroken vigil. In defying the government they were all risking two years' jail under the new Border Force Act, but defy they did.

I had visited a few days earlier, too, and what had struck me then was the breadth of locals there. I met grandparents Don and Patricia who had travelled ninety minutes each way on the bus just to be there, and I shared a meal with some local Rohingya refugees who had cooked for the protesters. Than, a Vietnamese refugee who ran a local café, had dropped in cakes, because, he said, 'Without opportunity I wouldn't be here.' The atmosphere then had been joyous, rebellious and full of hope as kids still in school uniforms chanted 'Let them stay'.

Ellen and I arrived at Lady Cilento Hospital late on the Friday afternoon to see a heaving mass of several hundred people circling it. There was a nervous energy and an air of defiance that was palpable. I had planned just to be a fellow protester, dressed as I was in shorts and a t-shirt. But Ellen, the incredible Natasha Blucher from the Darwin Asylum Seeker Support and Advocacy Network (DASSAN) and I quickly realised that the crowd was looking for some direction and leadership and, by accident, we were it.

The very first thing we identified was the hospital's many exits, and we quickly made sure that every one was covered by ready and willing people. But that wasn't enough.

I turned to Ellen. 'So how are we going to stop them if they try to move Asha and her mum?' We looked at each other, racking our brains. I could only think of one thing that might work.

I went around to every group at each exit and quietly asked each of the protesters if they would be willing to lie down in front of oncoming cars to stop their removal if necessary.

No one flinched. Everyone said yes. Fuck.

Next I sent out a tweet calling for even more peaceful protesters at Lady Cilento. It was so heartening to see that people just kept coming until our numbers were boosted to around five hundred. I had no speech planned but all these faces kept looking at me. So I stepped up onto a bench, took a breath and asked them two things. Firstly, if they were willing to be arrested for peacefully stopping the removal of Asha and her mum, and, if so, if they were also willing to surround and stop any car that looked like it could be moving them out of hospital.

Not one person said no.

Then I also asked that everyone be respectful of not interfering with the duties of the hospital, which meant no blocking ambulances or emergencies.

What came next was simply extraordinary. This huge group of people was one: it was united, defiant and ready to do whatever was needed. Everywhere I looked that night I saw humanity at its best – fearless and compassionate. I still get tingles thinking about it.

Over to my left I saw protesters peacefully stopping and surrounding police cars to make sure baby Asha was not being taken away. (I also want to say here that the police were respectful and understanding throughout the evening.) And over to my right the sky was proudly filled by a huge Aboriginal flag from the Seed Indigenous youth climate network with 'Let Them Stay' emblazoned on it, and alongside it various Australian flags flapped gently in solidarity, letting us know they had our backs.

All things indicated it was shaping up to be a long night, and at around 7.30 pm I realised we needed food to keep us going. I posted a tweet asking for pizza, hoping we might get a couple delivered to the hospital courtesy of locals in the immediate area. And indeed, a few arrived soon after and we were grateful. But then what happened completely blew me away. Taxi drivers and delivery drivers kept approaching me with pizza boxes saying that they had been told to give them to 'anyone holding a "Let Them Stay" sign'. It was just beautiful. Throughout the course of the evening, more than 250 pizzas were delivered, ordered and paid for by everyday Aussies from every capital city around our nation. On reflection I think people were desperate to do something, to be connected, and to show their solidarity and support. It felt like we had the whole nation behind us that night and it made us feel unstoppable. And, of course, we also shared the pizzas with the emergency staff at Lady Cilento, the Brisbane police and several local homeless shelters.

Deep into the night we got word that #LetThemStay was the number-four trending topic globally on Twitter,

ALL MY LIFE PEOPLE HAVE TOLD ME THAT I AM NAIVE FOR THINKING THAT LOVE IS A TRIUMPHANT FORCE, THAT COMPASSION CAN CONQUER ANYTHING AND THAT BEING VULNERABLE IS POWER. I AM HERE TO TELL YOU THAT ALL OF THESE THINGS ARE TRUE.

no small feat. The world was watching and the government was shitting itself. It truly felt like a night for people power. Next we learned that the AMA president, Michael Gannon, had tweeted that 'Any attempt to forcibly remove baby Asha [is] a dangerous act from which there is no return.' This got a huge roar from the crowd. Wow. Apparently Premier Annastacia Palaszczuk became personally involved too. At last we heard that the federal government had given its assurance not to move baby Asha and her mum.

Candles had been lit and then, somewhat spontaneously, we all sang 'Advance Australia Fair'. We sang it loudly and we sang it with pride, and it was the first time the words had really meant something to me in a long, long time. We had won the night because the protest belonged to everyone – it wasn't owned by anyone or any organisation – it sprang from the hearts of all caring and decent people.

All my life people have told me that I am naive for thinking that love is a triumphant force, that compassion can conquer anything and that being vulnerable is power. I am here to tell you that all of these things are true. And love transcends all, because when we lead with it we are at our best.

8

THE POWER OF LOVE

Martin Luther King wrote, 'Love is the most durable power in the world.' In some ways this four-letter word seems radical in our current times. Love refuses to kneel at the altar of self-interest and fear, and it refuses to be seduced by that which diminishes us. By this I am largely thinking of our political leaders, who urge us to care less and to engage less. They coax us instead to be angry that we have a social safety net for the poor, to be angry at refugees who cross the sea to save their lives, and to be afraid of young African Australians in your community who also dream of a safe and better life.

Yet it is love that we must turn to in times of hate, for hate is a dead-end for our souls and for society. It might seem quaintly old-fashioned to think so, but showing love for one another and leading with love is everything. Love inspires, while hate consumes us. In words both simple and powerful, the Reverend King also wrote, 'I have decided to stick with love. Hate is too great a burden to bear.'

Love uplifts us. It is the scaffolding of our humanity. It provides sanctuary to the oppressed because it sees them as human beings in need of welcome. Love asks, What would I want if my family knocked on the door of a stranger seeking refuge from harm? What would I want for my children for whom I had sacrificed all that we had known to bring them to safer shores?

Love asks, If I were to lose my job and become unemployed, would drug-testing me rehabilitate my hope of a new beginning? Would being punished for my poverty make me more willing to give back to society?

Love asks, If I lose my way and break the law, is locking me away with no regard for my own lifetime of trauma the best way forward? Love asks, Once I have served this sentence will I be a citizen ready to contribute and assimilate, or will I be filled with anger and hurt and take that out on my community again?

Love asks, If I give nothing back to the community what, apart from my own hubris and greed, will flourish? What will the next generation inherit?

Love sees each of us, all of us, as important, as worthwhile, as having a place at the table of equality, community and possibility.

LOVE SEES EACH
OF US, ALL OF US,
AS IMPORTANT, AS
WORTHWHILE, AS
HAVING A PLACE
AT THE TABLE
OF EQUALITY,
COMMUNITY AND
POSSIBILITY.

So love triumphs over everything. It is expansive, it is inclusive and it is everywhere. The Reverend King made its power clear: 'Everybody wishes to love and be loved. He who feels that he is not loved feels that he does not count.' That was definitely me in my earlier years. Although I knew my family loved me in so many ways, I still felt that I did not count.

As the questions above have established, there are many types of love. And there is one type in particular that is necessary for all of us, and that is the love of self. By that I don't mean self-interest or narcissism but rather a self-acceptance and a kindness to oneself. This is essential if we are to help each other. It is also something that I have struggled with for many years.

We all have our own addictions, our ways of coping with emotional hurt, loss, grief, low self-esteem and trauma. I know for many of us the tools we use to cope rarely nurture us and often just make the hurt worse by burying it just beneath the surface.

I had all the lights on in my bathroom. I didn't want there to be anywhere where the dark could save me at 1 am on that Monday morning. I stood naked in front of the mirror. I checked all the angles. I didn't want to have any side that might be forgiving. I wanted to see every sorry inch of me.

My hairy chest was thick like a wild Amazonian forest that knew nothing about borders. It ranged high up around my shoulders and to my back, and it crept all the way down to surround my pelvis. I had been ashamed of it since I was a child. Why couldn't I have been like the athletic, hairless Anglo men I grew up with and all the girls liked? Those boys' lives seemed so simple. Growing up I had thought they had the ideal body. That would have made all the difference.

I sighed and continued to scrutinise myself. I had man boobs. They're actually breasts, I decided, though they held no shape. I felt emasculated just looking at them. I knew it was because I was overweight, but that provided little comfort.

I looked down to my tummy. I was so bloated. I looked at my belly with such anger. I know it had grown so much from decades of self-loathing, of emotional eating, of loneliness. My bear-sized hands felt weak and fragile, but these were the hands that had betrayed my body. Hands that had fed me, not to fill me up but to keep me alone.

(I know that lots of women reading this know what I'm talking about, because the pressure for women is tenfold what it is for men. It starts by the time girls can walk, this sexist and oppressive unrealistic body size that women are taught to attain. Women are shamed for their bodies on an hourly basis and vulture capitalism preys on these insecurities. Just think of the judgmental and even scornful looks when women have 'eaten too much', or 'put on too much weight' – they are on a treadmill that never stops. The message sent is that women's value is all wrapped up in their bodies, it's on the tag that proclaims their size. How reductive. How nonsensical. Imagine if men were treated this way.)

I know as men we're told that we're not meant to talk about feeling like this, but that's exactly why men need to open up and be vulnerable. We need to abandon the idea of being a 'real man' because it does us real harm. Through most of my life I have struggled with my own body image and my relationship with food. I ate when I was lonely, I ate when I felt rejected, I ate when I felt worthless and overwhelmed, I ate to help myself sleep and I ate in the early hours of the morning. I ate until I was full many times over but still felt so empty. Somehow, though, I kept thinking I could fill that hole with food.

Our relationship with any addiction – be it to food, alcohol, drugs or gambling – is primarily an emotional one. The addiction in question does not judge us; instead it brings us instant (if temporary) relief. It releases our tensions and anxieties. It gives us comfort in times of need. And yet whenever I ate to compensate for what was missing inside me, I always felt remorse, anger and shame afterwards.

To the question of whether any woman could love me when I was so overweight, I already knew the answer was no. More importantly, though, was the fact that *I* could never love me. Not this fat, ugly piece of shit I saw in the mirror. And I hid behind it like it was my special armour. In my twenties I spent years wearing the same big grey overcoat, which was like my own magician's cape I could physically disappear into.

So how do we start to think of how we might like ourselves more, and even grow to love ourselves? We start with three simple words: I am enough.

Seriously, we need to shed our shame and be free of it. We are a society that shames us for suffering, that wants us to hide away our vulnerability behind walls of invisibility. We hide our ageing, our ill health, our suffering, our crisis. We shame those who look different, love differently, whose faith or skin colour does not match our own ideas of worth. We label, medicate, demonise, criminalise our suffering in such a way that to acknowledge it might weaken us, might rob us of a wholly fabricated invincibility.

There is nothing wrong with you, and whatever you are doing to cope with your trauma, be gentle on yourself. Know it is temporary and let go of judgment. If you are a survivor of sexual abuse or incest, I believe you. If you are wanting to come out, I support you. If you are battling an addiction, know you will find a nurturing way to heal and deserve help. If you are dealing with bullying or racism at school or work, know that you are not the problem. You are beautiful as you are.

We need more spaces to allow ourselves to ask for help. It's incredibly brave when people reach out and do just that, but it's also damning that often they feel they can't start by turning to people in their own lives for help. What does this say about us as a community?

For four years in the mid-1990s I spent Wednesday nights from midnight till around 4 am in a basement in West Melbourne as a volunteer telephone counsellor for Crisis Line. Although this organisation no longer exists, I clearly recall that all of the stories had a familiar ache to them: 'I want to die … I am going to kill myself … The pain is too much … I feel so alone … I have no one to talk to … I don't how I'm going to face another day … My partner hits me … I want to come out but I'm scared my family will disown me … Why won't this depression go away?'

This job showed me how many of us feel so alone, how many of us are shamed into silence and hide our pain out of fear of more rejection or judgment. It also showed me how much we need someone to listen to us, just to hear our pain, without judgment or blame, and to feel safe while we do it. We cannot heal if we don't have a little space that feels safe, without blame, fear or judgment.

That so many people felt they could only talk about their deepest pain, suffering, fears and grief to a stranger was something that stayed with me. Why do we feel so isolated from one another? Why are we so scared of letting people see that we are suffering and in pain? Why is pain shameful? Why is not coping shameful? Why do we have to pretend to be okay?

When nothing you do is good enough, it leaves a hole in you that is impossible to fill. Nothing will ever be good enough. It's likely that you feel inadequate in many situations or like an impostor. Perhaps you worry that you are going to disappoint people, and that people don't say how they really feel about you.

Yet we can't build a better world unless we're also building ourselves up, loving ourselves, cutting ourselves some slack. There can be no progress unless we have self-love and self-worth. We can't build better communities and homes and futures unless we are at the heart of it. How do we heal a society if we cannot heal ourselves? We can't have forgiveness, compassion, perspective and kindness for others if we don't have them for ourselves.

We're always apologising for our desires and dreams. But what if we stopped trying to *win* and instead just tried to connect and be part of something deeper and real?

My greatest desire is to feel safe. I crave safety and yet for most of my life it has eluded me. My life has always seemed so mercurial and changeable. It would be great not to have to feel that I always needed to be in control, be strong, have it together. It makes me feel incredibly alone to have to appear strong all the time. And yet when I have been vulnerable and open in the past, I have often been hurt and betrayed by the people I thought I could count on. And that in turn made (and still makes) me feel even more pathetic and stupid for allowing myself to get so close to people and to trust them. And so the cycle continues ... To be honest, though, I think I'm getting better at it, and it does take a lot of practice and trust in yourself.

We all have our own battles to fight and I know many of you are dealing with far tougher issues than mine. I want to ask you to start where I have started, which is in a place with no judgment and no blame. This place also asks for patience and acceptance of yourself and, with that, forgiveness.

Having no judgment means that I reassure myself that I am not a fuck-up for doing the very things that make me feel more worthless. I am doing the best I can, and when I do things that hurt me it's a self-preservation strategy, my way of managing my anxiety, fears and self-doubt. None of this makes me a bad person – it just makes me human.

Having no blame means accepting that who I am in this moment and what I am struggling with has many roots, paths and contributors, but that right now I need to let go of blame, no matter who might be responsible. I need to accept that those who have caused my hurt either don't care or don't know how to work through it with me, even if they wanted to. Perhaps they don't have the tools, self-awareness or even the space to have looked at these issues before. Ultimately, I have to deal with this on my own.

Having patience means knowing I haven't got it all figured yet. I still struggle with my confidence and self-esteem, I still mess up, but I am growing, learning and always doing the best I can. I can't ask any more than that for myself.

Having acceptance means knowing that I will always feel a little like a freak, like I don't ever truly belong or make sense, and that's okay; I actually don't want to fit in and conform. The flaws I have are what make me human and real; they're also what make me unique.

Having forgiveness for myself means that I understand that at the time I was doing my best. I know that's so much easier said than felt, but over the years I have had to slowly learn to forgive myself rather than continue my masochistic merry-go-round of regret and self-loathing.

We are human and we do the best we can in any situation, thinking we're making the right decision.

KINDNESS IS TRANSFORMATIVE.

It's only with the benefit of hindsight that we realise other options were available. In forgiving myself I'm acknowledging that when things went to shit in the past, it wasn't because I willingly chose unhappiness or heartbreak or disappointment or loneliness. I was just doing the best I could to keep it together and get through that moment.

Even if you have done things in the past that were destructive and you hurt yourself and people you cared about, you can't heal and try to make things right with people you have wronged without first starting with yourself.

Kindness is transformative. We all respond to kindness. It brings out the best in us, and sends out a positive energy that nurtures and inspires others to do the same. When we're kind to others we rise above the cynical politics of the day and say, 'We are better and we can do better.'

For more than a quarter of a century I have helped people with complex needs and issues, people who have been in prison, people who are homeless and drug-affected, and not once has anyone harmed me. I have always felt safe because I have always tried to lead with kindness.

If you're still struggling with forgiving yourself, here are some small acts of kindness that might help.

EXPECT THINGS FROM YOURSELF

One of the cruellest things we can do is set our own expectations so low that we can't disappoint ourselves.

When we have no or very low expectations of ourselves – because we have been raised not to, told not to, or have internalised the hate, discrimination, homophobia or bullying that we have experienced – we have already forsaken hope. Such an existence is not a true life, and nothing beautiful and powerful can come from punishing your heart and spirit in this way.

KNOW YOU MATTER

If you are feeling adrift, isolated and alone, I want you to know that you are loved and that you matter. We all do. So many people struggle with just keeping on living. I get that. I understand feeling overwhelmed with despair and an unrelenting desire for the pain to stop at any cost. But I want you to know that as dark as it may seem right now and as low and powerless as you may feel, there is hope. That hope is in all of us and we all need each other to make it really happen. We all matter.

REMEMBER: WE ARE NOT MEANT TO BE ALONE

When you are low, don't judge your coping mechanisms and the dark thoughts that prevail – these are your survival strategies and they have got you to this point. No matter how worthless or weak you feel, remember that you are a survivor. You are still here and you are doing the best you can. Sometimes it takes everything we have just to keep the show on the road and pretend things are okay while we have chaos within us.

So often we fear that people will not accept us, want us, need us, care for us and love us if they see all of us. We think that no one will want us if there are flaws and emotional wear and tear. And part of the reason for that is we don't accept ourselves. We so rarely ask for help because we don't think we have a right to it. Let people in. Ask for help. You are worth it.

We need our stories to be heard and our pain acknowledged, and to know we are safe and can find a way forward, no matter how slowly. Be in that moment, reclaim your story, your voice. Find it for yourself. The hurt, fear, history and trauma are part of you too. You don't need to pretend that they're not there, but remember they're not a signpost to where everything's going to end up, just an indication of where in the road you last hit a bump.

9
EMBRACING YOUR FEARS

The stage lights were bearing down on me. I hadn't expected it to be so hot on the small stage. The Brunswick Green room was bursting with punters, and it was never meant for stand-up comedy. Before tonight it had only ever seen avant-garde jazz singers and university students in search of young love on three pints. The room connects right to the bar; there was no door so the risk of hecklers was high.

Over one hundred people were crammed into a room built for sixty, many there to see me perform. I had wanted to prove to myself that I could do anything I put my mind to, that I didn't have to be afraid of anything. A stand-up comedy show was in my Top 3 of things that most terrified me. That's why, in 2010, I was up on that stage.

I had created a one-hour, one-man show called *The Hateful Humanitarian* for the Melbourne International

Comedy Festival. The tagline was something like 'It's not easy being a humanitarian. People expect you to love everything. I don't.' So there I was at thirty-seven years of age about to share pretty much every embarrassing moment in my life. I was tired of being ashamed. I was tired of hiding all my awkwardness and my lies about how I felt about myself. I had this idea that if I said it out loud and shared it with total strangers, it meant that I'd taken control and that I had freed myself from it. I knew from many years of suffering just how shame flourishes in the silence.

And so I told the audience about my life. I started with my tormented adolescence, about how I had a thicker moustache than most of my high school teachers, and that mine at twelve rivalled Dennis Lillee's. That I had a monobrow that looked like a giant caterpillar had died on my forehead, and that I was so hairy a *National Geographic* crew wanted to film me, convinced they had finally found a yeti.

I joked about how my teenage years were a sexual wasteland, although rumours spread far and wide about my sexual exploits with a female by the name of Mitsy. Mitsy was my silky black labrador.

I shared tales about my tragic dating life, including being on RSVP where I had the super sexy moniker of JellyBelly Heart (melding my love of jelly beans with my big belly). I also, somewhat unkindly, spoke of women I dated whose profile photos were taken before the fall of the Berlin Wall. I even did a ribbon dance routine to 'Take My Breath Away' from the *Top Gun* soundtrack, a pastiche of my failed attempts to woo women. I laughed at my hairy back and at my hopeless attempts to tame it – from bleaching to waxing to shaving. I told them how my back once turned a bright yellow from using a skin bleaching cream and how it glowed in the dark afterwards. I said that I was so hairy there were parts of my body that even God hadn't seen, and that when it came to shopping for grooming products I had to go to Bunnings.

Then I turned to family. I joked about my aunt who had thought I would be in jail as an adult, a call she made when I was just five years old (I have never forgotten that). And my other aunt who, no matter how much my mum praised my achievements ('My son is a lawyer') would respond with, 'I know taxi drivers with law degrees.' I shared the story of a family friend who bragged about their son who had finally completed a course, and they had the certificate framed and proudly displayed in the hallway of their home. Sadly, it was for completing an anger management course.

I laughed about how my mum was so proud of me but when she seemed down and I would ask her, 'What's wrong?' she would then unload in a way ethnic kids knew only too well: 'What do you mean what's wrong? You're thirty-seven, unmarried, a vegetarian, and you care more about the refugees than your own mother. What have I done to deserve this? What did I do wrong?' Ethnic mums do guilt so well it's an art form. In fact, I wouldn't be surprised if their playbook of guilt now comes as an app.

I had a great time telling the audience how my mum thought she could get away with anything in Greek in front of girlfriends and they would not catch on despite the dirty looks, raised voice and endless swear words. Thankfully she stopped doing that in my thirties. My mum was also my own personal smart-traveller warning service any time I went on a holiday, as anxious about me going to Daylesford as she was me going to New Delhi. I talked about the special ways that I bond with my mother and how we share a love of violent action films, especially those of Jean-Claude Van Damme, where she loudly chants, 'Finish him! Finish him!' as each villain is killed.

I spoke about my dear, beautiful cousin who was forty-four and unmarried. And then, with a complexity that Einstein would have been proud of, I used a whiteboard to map out how old she really was in Greek years. Years were added for weight, the number of Australian boyfriends she previously had and her eating habits. From my calculations it transpired that her real age in Greek years was 172. That's how cruel and mean we are to ethnic women over forty.

I laughed about the guy who rang the ASRC to donate his little sailboat that could carry four people.

When I accepted the offer, he hesitated and asked for more information before suddenly having a change of heart.

'Why,' I asked? 'What's the issue? The refugees I work with will enjoy going fishing in this boat.'

'Sorry, I can't be part of it.'

'What do you mean you can't be part of it?'

'I can't be a part of people smuggling and have you use my boat to smuggle refugees from Indonesia.'

I kid you not.

I made fun about other donations too – tennis rackets with no strings, shoes with holes in them, G-strings with the devil's face on them and cans of hummus ten years out of date.

The crowd cheered and laughed – thankfully *with* me, not *at* me – throughout the night. When I had finished the first show, I felt a sense of elation I have rarely felt in my life. And it *was* as if, for a moment, all the shit that had shamed me, crushed me, defined me was gone. I felt invincible! I went on to do three sold-out seasons of *The Hateful Humanitarian*, raising forty thousand dollars for the ASRC from 2010 to 2012. In the last year I grew so much in confidence I was doing 7 pm and 10 pm shows most nights.

How I ended up on that stage is a much longer story.

In my twenties I was so convinced that I could never, ever be loved that I closed myself off from women. I thought no woman could love me, desire me, want me. There were a couple of women who had tried to show some interest, but I was either oblivious to this or chose not to recognise it, too scared of what it would mean for me to acknowledge it and to act on it. To let someone in. I used to push people away before they got too close, because once anyone got to know the real me, how could they possibly still want to be with me? I felt like an impostor so I couldn't afford for people to see me as I really was.

The older I got the more trapped I felt. As a man I felt like a freak. I remember my sister taking me to a restaurant in Richmond on my birthday where a group of my friends was sitting at a table – it was a surprise birthday party for me. My very first response was to think, What a coincidence they're all here tonight. That's how little I expected of me and how little I thought others felt about me.

By the time I hit my thirties I felt like such a fraud. There I was, a social worker and a lawyer telling people to be brave, not to lose hope or give up, to take risks and find their happiness, while I was hiding away from the world. I was paralysed by my fears – that I would always be alone, that I was too unlovable to be desired by anyone, ever. I was so scared of everything – from touch, to intimacy, to telling someone that I had feelings for them. Everything filled me with dread and panic, and the expectation that I would only ever be rejected. I had to face the ugly truth that I was a coward who was afraid of everything and anything outside of my work. The reality was that nobody could have hated me more, disowned me more or hurt me more than I had already done. *I* was the problem here, and the only way out of this emotional and spiritual abyss was for me to start taking responsibility for myself. The only other alternative, I thought, was to end everything.

Now, let me just say that I didn't want to die, but at that point I had no hope for the future. Thankfully I knew that I was at rock bottom, and I knew that my life was in danger unless I asked for help and really made an effort to change things. Honestly, I had no set plan, but I did know, with every part of me, that I could no longer wake up to each day with things as they were.

How was I ever going to love anyone, have a relationship, start a family if I could not love myself? There was no way I was ever going to have intimacy, a genuine connection or even deep friendships without love for myself. And I also had no right to encourage others to love and believe in themselves if I couldn't do the same. We need to work at being happy. We need to face our fears. So just like when I was eighteen and knew I had to change and grow, I knew I had to face these fears and not turn away.

I have always been awkward socially. I can stand in front of ten thousand people and speak, but you'd find it difficult to speak to me face to face at a party, mostly because I'll be hiding in a corner with a drink, trying to shrink from everyone's sight. I just get lost for words; socially, I'm such a dork.

Can you relate to that? Where you are able to be anything – confident, strong, assertive, someone who leads and believes in others – for everyone else but yourself? Give encouragement and build people up while you quietly tear yourself down? It's exhausting, isn't it? To have to channel all your energy into just trying to appear normal on the outside while inside it's turmoil.

But I made a promise to myself. I knew I had to rewrite my story. Reframe it. Reaffirm it. I had to change things and I started to take risks, small ones to start.

I began by asking one person to be my friend and then being surprised when they said yes, which gave me confidence to ask a second, and another. (When you put that positive energy out there it really does feed itself and draw people to you.) I had also decided to be honest about myself, to share who I was and how I was feeling, with no filter and no bullshit. I was tired of being a fraud. To my surprise and delight, it drew more and more people to me. I guess they reckoned that they could likewise be themselves with me, that they didn't need to censor and edit themselves or appear to have it all together. Instead, they could be complex, messy, strong, vulnerable, anxious, warm, humble, loving, strong and fragile all at once. And I adored them for it! It was such a beautiful gift. I was able to bring my warmth, gentleness and sincerity to my relationships and as people showed me love I was able to start to believe it and receive it. It was incredibly healing for me.

I learned that it was okay not to make sense, that it was okay to be an outlier, and I soon realised that all the best people are the freaks, those who also don't fit into round holes. They are my people. Don't let being different shame you or break you; let it make you.

The biggest development in my self-love journey was that finally I had my first intimate relationship at the age of thirty-two. For such a long time I was so deeply ashamed of this fact. I want to share it now because our grief, hurt and trauma *don't* define us, and I refuse to let me shame myself any more. I don't care how that makes me look as a man either. I have no interest in being a 'real man'; I just want to be a kind and decent one. Love came to me and me to love when I was ready and able to receive it. It was beyond wonderful! And while I still have some grief about missing out on all of that in my twenties, I remain truly grateful to have experienced love deeply and sincerely. So bless the lovely soul who bravely took the initiative and pashed me one night at the local pub after losing patience for me to make the first move. I will always be grateful to

DON'T LET BEING DIFFERENT SHAME YOU OR BREAK YOU; LET IT MAKE YOU.

her for seeing something in me, for she became my first love. And the woman I lost my virginity to. There, I've said it. I was thirty-two when I lost my virginity.

Over the next decade I followed my heart and made myself vulnerable. I let women I cared for know how I felt. To stand there and tell a woman how I felt about her was absolutely terrifying. I had to keep telling myself it was okay to be a mess and scared, that it was not a weakness to share how I was feeling and to talk about my emotions.

Sure, there were times when it didn't go as I hoped and I ended up on the kitchen floor with a bottle of red and Ani DiFranco's 'Untouchable Face' on repeat, berating myself with, What was I thinking? and, My heart will never get over this, but it did. And I put myself back out there again and again. The really big thing was that at last I had reached a point in my life where I believed I could be loved. I was worthy of love. So each time I stood in front of a woman, vulnerable and fragile, at that moment I had actually never been stronger. No matter what happened next, I had never been truer to myself.

If you're struggling to believe you can be loved as you are now, know that you can be. How do I know this? Because we're all worth loving and we all deserve love. Allowing yourself to be loved means letting people decide for themselves whether to love you, not you doing it for them. Whether it's reciprocated or not, expressing your love is part of being human; it's how we connect to another. And it's as necessary to us as breathing is. Yes, it will bring hurt and rejection at times, but it will also bring something wondrous when you're in love and feel loved and love yourself.

Around this time, too, I started to work less and spend more time with family and friends. I started to expand my life through travel, and I reconnected to pleasure and happiness just for me. I started to unlearn how to be a man. I stopped pretending that I was strong, had my shit together and was in control. I let go of some of my shame and I started to surround myself with people who understood and liked me.

I also went on the most incredible journeys over the next decade, including visiting forty countries. I climbed Mount Kilimanjaro with no training and trekked to Machu Picchu. I almost died in the Himalayan mountains in a snowstorm with Nola. I rode on the roof of a bus in Nepal, savoured pistachio vanilla ice cream in the old souks of Damascus, wandered for days through Petra, rode camels on Christmas Eve into the Sahara Desert then camped under the stars, ate street food in Hanoi on hot summer nights, tangoed (well, tried to) in Buenos Aires,

My friend Gavin and me with our two guides after a five-day hike to the top of Mount Kilimanjaro, Tanzania, in 2011.

took cooking classes in Cambodia, swam in the deep blue seas of the Greek island Amorgos, got badly sunburned on Copacabana beach, walked along the Great Wall of China and saw pandas in Chengdu.

I ate momos and visited the Potala Palace in Tibet, smoked pot in Amsterdam, walked up the ancient Red Pyramid in Cairo, listened to jazz in New York, swam in Ha Long Bay in Vietnam, went to the World Cup in Germany, visited Auschwitz (which profoundly affected me), rode white-water rapids in Laos and Uganda, went on a wildlife safari in the Serengeti (and got stranded there when our car broke down), ate goulash in Budapest and pakoras in Jaipur, joined an Indian wedding in Bundi, celebrated New Year's Eve with wine on Las Ramblas in Barcelona, practised yoga in Ubud and sat on a park bench in Istanbul between the Hagia Sophia and the Blue Mosque during prayer time and drank it all in.

But as well as grand overseas adventures, I also took the time to explore new things closer to home. I had never been able to run more than a couple of kilometres before, so I set myself the challenge of running a half-marathon. I asked others to join me in support of refugees and came up with Run 4 Refugees, a charity run for the ASRC that has raised well over one million dollars. The second year I ran the half-marathon in under two hours, and I've completed seven more since.

I have always wanted to be far more creative, and so I tried my hand at being a painter, sculptor, photographer and documentary filmmaker. I co-directed and acted in my first ever short film, which makes Tommy Wiseau's *The Room* look like a Billy Wilder film. I was a villainous immigration officer in *Journey of Asylum*, a play about the journeys of refugees that had a season at Trades Hall in 2010. I also had a go at learning French and salsa dancing. Another real desire of mine was to overcome my body image issues, so I did the most confronting things I could think of to face my fears: I became a qualified massage therapist, started yoga, and shared my love of Greek cooking by running cooking classes. I also opened for Circus Oz in a special performance that aimed to help people seeking asylum and to raise funds for the ASRC. I was absolutely scared shitless as I was lowered some twenty metres from the 'sky' dressed as a Greek god, with a harness around me and hard wooden floor below me. Then, once I was on the ground, I used my Thor hammer to break the chains of a huge box and release a group of refugee children who had been trapped inside. The crowd simply roared!

Each of these experiences was life-affirming and made me feel so present in my life. At last I felt like I was finally living it and working it all out just for me and no one else. And I learned that we need to run towards fear, not away from it. Often fear is something we desire but believe ourselves unworthy of having, of experiencing. Surely it's better to be fearless, passionate, vulnerable, messy, complex and compassionate than to be ordinary? Surely we should all really live our lives as fully as we can?

Embracing your fear means following your heart in all parts of life. And you can start anywhere. Right here, right now – start with the smallest thing that makes you scared.

I know it's hard to let your long-held patterns and the past go. It's because you then have to face the grief of the life not lived. And with it the realisation that it could have been different so much sooner. The grief is often too much to let in, so we double down on the status quo. Forgive yourself and know you could not have come to this point sooner as you were in self-preservation mode.

10

THERE IS ALWAYS HOPE IN CHAOS

I have often found that the darker it gets, the greater the opportunity is for us to show the light, be the light, find a way through the darkness and chaos. Wherever there is chaos, there is hope.

I have already written about the hand-to-mouth existence of the ASRC and of how we've generally winged it from month to month over the years, so heavily dependent on the time, effort and financial support of others. Back in 2014 it really looked as if the writing was on the wall – the ASRC was about to become homeless. Our landlord for the previous seven years was kicking us out, and we were on a monthly lease so we could have been booted out onto the streets pretty much at any time. It's true, too, that our rent was far below the market value, but that was only going to make things more difficult for us. To find a building of the same size in West Melbourne or central Melbourne would have meant a rent increase of as much as 600 per cent. It would be the end of us.

But we knew that if we did go under, so too would a critical lifeline for around three thousand people who were seeking asylum at the time. Thousands of lives were potentially at stake.

As luck would have it we found a building in Footscray, just thirty metres from our very first address when we opened back in 2001. It felt so right to be back where it had all started and to be close to so many refugee communities in Melbourne. The building itself, however, was a total dump. The upstairs had been unoccupied for the last ten years and the ground floor was a filthy, dilapidated rabbit warren, untenanted for more than three years. It was going to cost at least eight million dollars to refit it, while we had a budget of eight hundred thousand. We had twelve weeks to get the main floor ready, which was 1,800 square metres, around the same size as seven tennis courts. Thankfully the ground floor was only 1,200 square metres, and again we had twelve weeks to get that ready. The reality was that this was a huge job that would normally take well over a year to complete – we had six months.

On board we had some wonderful companies, led by the National Australia Bank, that worked at mates' rates and donated so much of their time. But even so, without a small army of people to help us, we weren't going to be able to complete these renovations. So once again I turned to social media – Facebook and Twitter – and asked for help. I asked the public to come and help us build our new home of hope. I had no idea what to expect.

Over the next six months more than six hundred people I had never met before came to our aid. There were in total thirty-nine working bees, forty massive dumpsters, and thousands of sandwiches made and donated to give us the energy to keep going. The people who came to help ranged from entire families with children as young as six to people well into their eighties. People of every generation and background rolled up their sleeves and got to work. Newly arrived refugees worked alongside uni students, mums and dads and grandparents. Some days there were more than a hundred of us, all covered in dust, dirt and grime from demolition work. Together we tore down walls, cut cables, ripped out ruined carpets, laid carpets, painted walls, carried hundreds of pieces of furniture up and down stairs. And through it all, everywhere I looked, I saw big smiling faces, even when they were all covered in dust or paint, or people were standing in dumpsters full of rubbish. You couldn't wipe those big grins off their faces no matter what. It was so humbling and inspiring, and it still fills my heart thinking about it.

Throughout the six months I kept asking people what brought them there and the answers were the same – they were tired of feeling helpless, tired of the cruelty towards refugees, tired of the inhumanity. 'I just want to help, I want to be part of something good, I want to show refugees that most Australians are good and care.'

Unbelievably, the ASRC's new home was completed on time and on budget. Once again it had been saved by the kindness of others, something that has happened *hundreds* of times. This care and kindness for others is always humbling and inspiring, and my gratitude again goes out to all of you who helped.

More recently the ASRC suffered another setback. Around a year ago we faced a huge humanitarian crisis when seven and a half thousand people across the country who had been waiting for up to four years just to be allowed to apply for asylum were suddenly informed that they now had a few scant months to do so. These people had no means to pay a lawyer and the application process itself was so labyrinthine that any lawyer would find it difficult. The ASRC urgently needed five more lawyers to help as many of these thousands of people as possible. We needed to find half a million dollars in fourteen days, something that even I thought was a long shot. To appeal to the wider community I knew we had to speak from the heart, tell the human story, show the injustice and let people see the scale of the human crisis. Four days later we had hit our target, thanks to the generosity of tens of thousands of people. With call after call, the same words were echoed: 'I want to keep a family safe,' 'I want to help,' 'This is outrageous and I know the ASRC will keep its promises.'

Because of this tsunami of kindness from everyday people, 891 people seeking asylum – every single one on our waiting list – were kept safe from danger.

In 2017 the ASRC was particularly reliant on people's generosity. On World Refugee Day we hoped to pass the previous year's total and raise three hundred thousand dollars. That sum would enable us to double the number of people we were housing, employ more mental health social workers and feed more families. Within eighteen hours a record $660,661 was donated, not just from across Australia but from all corners of the globe. We had ninety-two-year-old Sister Mary who sent fifty dollars in a tissue, and one person who, down to their last forty-five dollars, sent us more than half of it because 'the refugees need it more than me'. I took calls from London, Bali, Bangkok, Fiji and Washington DC, all of them from concerned Australians who, no matter where they were now living across the globe, had not forgotten the shame of what our government was doing to refugees.

Last year we ran out of rice in our food bank, which is like bread for the people we assist. I put out a tweet asking for donations of rice, and within forty-eight hours one tonne of rice had been delivered. Another time we had run out of honey, instant coffee, dishwashing liquid and tuna, and again I went to social media and asked people to order online. The major supermarket chain we directed people to gave us a call and asked us to let them know next time we were running a food appeal. Apparently, three of their largest branches had completely sold out of the items we had requested from our supporters. That is the power of goodness in action.

This is why, after so many years working for refugees' rights, I am still hopeful. The more the debate has soured, the greater the humanitarian response from the Australian community has become. We are a minority as a refugee movement but we are, as I like to say, a minority of millions who refuse to be silent. The worse the debate becomes, the more people from every generation and background come through our doors. I see this at every packed house each time we hold a volunteer information night. Just a week ago we booked out 350 places for our volunteer night within a few days, and it's been like that since we opened.

The people who volunteer with us are not full-time activists (contrary to the caricatures that are trotted out by right-wing media and politicians); they are everyday mums and dads, doctors, carpenters, lawyers, teachers, musicians, accountants, students, engineers, nurses, businesspeople – in short, they are people from every walk of life.

Indeed, our volunteers and donors span every generation, and their small acts of kindness show people at their best, especially the youngsters. They include nine-year-old Ella, who with her friends swam for twelve hours (1,200 laps) to raise ten thousand dollars for the ASRC; and Walid, a refugee imprisoned on Manus who gave thirty dollars – his entire phone credit for a month, forfeiting his only connection to the outside world – to our winter appeal. They are children like little Sebastian, who at eight saved his pocket money for three months to buy food for refugees. It's difficult to describe the warm feeling I got watching his own delight in stacking the shelves with groceries he'd paid for. It's seen with five-year-old Argenta, who along with her donation sent a drawing with the words 'you are very beautiful and I love you'; and with Alice, who, together with fellow ten-year-olds baked and sold goodies at the Preston Market to raise $1,036 for the ASRC.

I see the best of us in people like pensioner Stephen Roberts, who has donated from his pension every fortnight for the last fifteen years. His only request is that we put it to good use helping in his words 'our people who are treasures'. It's in Sister Rita, a Catholic nun who has volunteered at our centre since 2003; and Sherrine Clark, one of the original students who started the ASRC with me and who then returned to lead our humanitarian services with unwavering dedication, which are at the coalface of daily crises. It's people like Peter McNamara, who wanted a job of meaning and purpose and so took a 70 per cent pay cut to become our general manager and who helped build the ASRC in its formative years; and Jana Favero, who has fearlessly led our advocacy programs for the past eight years. I saw it in the tireless work of the late Dorothy Kingston, a firebrand of a human being who volunteered for a decade while well into her eighties, helping us with everything from lobbying the state government to watering the plants, may she rest in peace.

All of these people have a social and moral conscience; they know we can be better and they themselves do better. And yes, we may be a minority but we are a minority of millions.

For years the community has rallied around refugees. Our friends are many and I have a special gratitude for the help of former prime minister Malcolm Fraser. It was such an honour to call Mr Fraser a friend, a man who was willing to risk his political capital and legacy to do what was morally right and to speak out fearlessly on behalf of refugees.

So many people told me the ASRC couldn't survive, that it was impossible for it to succeed as an organisation without accepting federal funding. The more people told

YES, WE MAY BE A MINORITY, BUT WE ARE A MINORITY OF MILLIONS.

me this, the more determined I became to prove them wrong. I kept thinking that the only way this place fails is if I give up, and there's no way I'm ever doing that. This is the struggle fought by my grandparents as refugees and my parents as migrants. This is why I fight, this is why it's in my blood, why I will keep fighting until refugees are free and safe. And this is how I knew the ASRC would be okay too – it's in the blood.

11

HOW TO BE A MAN

'You fucken dirty wog!' bellowed a mullet-headed man from a clapped-out red Toyota.

The car stopped and circled back towards me. It was a sunny Sunday afternoon in suburbia and I was out for an afternoon walk.

'Wooooogg!' he taunted. 'This is *my* country. Go back to your own country, arsehole!'

Just to make sure I didn't miss a word, he had poured himself out of the car window while screaming at me and his shitty baseball cap had fallen off. I picked it up and kept walking, looking for a rubbish bin to dump it into, my small act of defiance.

The car circled back again.

'Give me back my fucken cap.'

The car stopped and, while his mate looked on, the driver got out and ambled over towards me. He was brandishing a big metal steering-wheel lock, presumably to clock me with.

Fuck it, I thought to myself, and threw back the cap. I started walking again, hoping that was the end of it.

About fifty metres away, his abuse started up again. But this time something in me just broke. I was no longer that little kid in primary school who copped abuse every week and had to suck it up.

Uh-uh. No more. I was done with that.

'C'mon then, you bastards!' I turned and screamed at them, almost frothing at the mouth. 'I'll take you both on. C'mon, you *fuckers*! Let's go!'

My heart almost burst out of my chest. I hadn't been in a fight since I was fourteen, and nearly twenty years later, here I was begging for one. I couldn't believe my rage. It just poured out of me – years of it, every racist slight I had endured since kindergarten. It was white-hot anger that had been bottled up for years and there seemed no end to it. I didn't have any concern what the outcome would be, I just wanted to hit them – hard, and repeatedly. As I continued to shout, the two men got scared and – like all racists, who are all cowards – got back into the car and drove off while still mouthing obscenities.

Thinking about it now, rage and violence towards others seems to be increasingly more common. But hate begets hate and it consumes you if you allow it to.

How should we men deal with such moments? How can we do better?

To this day I'm still often abused and bullied, if in a slightly different fashion. I have more than two thousand names on my Twitter block list and here are some actual examples of what some of these men write to me:

> Fuck you Cunt. Hopefully next time your throat gets slashed ... Kon I hope you get terrorist attacked on you and your family then you'll realise Pauline [Hanson] is a saint ... I hope you get hung up with a rope on a tree by someone, you have it coming to you ... You *cuck*, *mangina*, poofter, faggot ... None of these women are going to fuck you Kon for playing the White Knight ... How dare you come to our already built country you bludging wog and think you have some voice?

I have been subjected to names and insults like these since I was a child, and luckily I haven't cared too much about what these types of boys and men have thought of me then and now. I suspect the main reasons for not caring so much comes from not having had a male peer group when younger, being a loner, and being drawn to friendships with women. When men troll me these days I say to them, 'Call me a pussy/*cuck*/*mangina*/faggot. Bring it. I don't give a damn.' And when men use the C word, thinking they're insulting me by comparing me to a woman's body, I say, 'So you're saying that I have warmth and depth, why thank you. :-)'

I suspect that the rage these men online feel springs from them believing that I have broken some unspoken rule, that I'm a traitor to my gender for speaking up for the rights of women, refugees, First Nations people and Australian Muslims. I am absolutely certain we have a crisis of masculinity where men don't seem to know what being a man means, and over the past twenty-seven years I have seen first-hand the terrible price men and, especially, women have paid and still pay for it.

And when I say that it's a crisis, I mean it. For that reason I'm not going to start small here.

Back in the 1990s, on Monday nights at the Jika Jika Community Centre in Northcote, I was regularly surrounded by a group of men who told their stories, often for the first time to anyone. They all had something in common apart from being male – they were all survivors of incest, child abuse or rape. The stigma of 'this doesn't happen to men' and 'if it did they must be a perpetrator too' had silenced these men for decades.

My role was to help co-facilitate the support group with incredible men like Dez Wildwood, Timothy O'Leary and Rod, who were themselves survivors. I had become friends with these amazing men when I was eighteen through an organisation called Men Against Sexual Assault. A couple of years later Dez founded a separate group called Non-Offending Male Survivors of Sexual Assault, the first support group of its kind anywhere in Australia. And so from the age of twenty I had the incredible honour of helping to run these meetings for these brave men for the next few years.

Adam was raised to be a devout Catholic in a home that was deeply religious. And this was largely why many years had passed before Adam revealed that he had been sexually abused by his father. He had always been told this is 'just how love is shown to you' and that 'God loves you and this is part of it'. I remember Adam sitting there clutching his cup of instant coffee but looking relieved that, finally, he had found a place where he would be believed and feel safe.

The gist of what these survivors shared was so often repeated from man to man: 'You're the first person I've told this to in thirty years', 'I've kept it to myself since I was five and I'm fifty now', 'I never thought anyone would believe me', 'My own siblings wouldn't let me near their children once I told them I was abused as a child', 'I spent my whole life thinking it was my fault, that I did something wrong for Dad to do this to me', 'Tonight is the first time I've felt safe enough to say this', and 'Hearing that I'm not alone means everything to me'.

Some of these men had spent most of their lives riven with guilt, thinking that they were villains when they were the victims of abuse from predatory male relatives or other men in positions of power. The real perpetrators varied in their roles, but it was frequently the man's father, uncle, grandfather or teacher; most often it was his priest, but also occasionally it was his mother.

There are so many myths surrounding male abuse – that men can't be raped, that it doesn't happen to real men, that men are always in control, that if they were physically aroused they must have wanted it and enjoyed it, and that if they were abused it followed that they too would become an abuser. What's important to realise here is that these *are* myths, founded on a fantasy grounded in dysfunctional masculinity, and they're so harmful to male survivors of abuse.

The reality is men *do* get raped. One in four children who are sexually abused are boys. And it's important to note that a victim of abuse does not necessarily become a perpetrator of it later in life. There is always a choice. It's also quite common for boys and men being abused to have an erection and to ejaculate, but don't think that this indicates a willingness to engage in the act and that it's consensual; on the contrary, it's an uncontrollable physiological reaction and a response to fear and panic. Men of all shapes, ages, size and sexuality are sexually assaulted, and men don't ask for it any more than a woman does. And in the same way that women are sexually abused by men, male rape is about power, control and dominating someone. What's especially important for us to acknowledge here as well is that we rarely teach boys about consent, and, more often than not, boys have little or no sense of where the boundaries are for both themselves and for others.

The most dangerous place for a boy growing up is, as it is for girls, the family home. There they are in the hands of the people they know and trust. The greatest harm we do to boys and men is to tell them that this could never happen to them. In doing so, if something dreadful does happen, we make them feel there is no safe space to share their stories.

So as Adam's tale illustrates, at least until recently, many boys were likely raised in the family home or church with the damning messages that such behaviour was how so-and-so showed his love or, conversely, that they must have been asking for it, or deserved it, or that they must be gay. I'm sure we all agree that these responses are wrong in so many ways. But when the person who abuses others is in a position of authority and a trusted figure, the person being abused may find it difficult to believe that this upstanding person would ever harm them. And this rationale, combined with the victim-blaming culture and stigma, is what silences so many survivors, sometimes for an entire lifetime.

For any men reading this who are survivors of rape, know that you are resilient, courageous and on a journey of recovery. You deserve love and safety and to be believed and supported. Try to remove any judgment attached to this trauma – from how much you can or can't remember, when it happened, what you are doing to cope, whether you have told others, and whether it's left you with questions around your sexuality. Take as much time as you need to heal, but please ask for help – it's there if you need it and you most certainly deserve it.

Two decades after my Monday nights in Northcote, I was busy with my fortnightly free massage clinic for homeless men at Ozanam House in North Melbourne. Each man here, too, had his own story of hurt, hope and loss. One by one they came into my makeshift massage room. I tried to compensate for the fact that my massage table was squashed right next to a beige office desk by draping the table with fresh crisp sheets for every massage. I thought they would help give the men the dignity they deserved.

One man almost limped into the room. He couldn't have been much older than me but he looked as if he'd suffered the hardships of several men. He glanced at me, slightly uncertain, and then sheepishly spoke. 'Hi, I'm Jack.' He nodded at his body. 'I was beaten up by the police and then attacked by some other blokes,' he said. 'I've, ah, been sleeping rough for the last few weeks and I'm sore everywhere.'

'Just lie down,' I said gently. 'Let's see if we can get rid of some of this pain for you.'

He sighed, sat on the table to take off his shirt and then lay down on his tummy. His naked back revealed a tale of stunning neglect with its discolouration, marks and scars, and the way it puckered in places. And once I touched him I learned a good deal more from the way the skin and muscles resisted my hands when I first began. The extremely deep knots of muscle in his back all indicated a huge burden of anxiety and tension. His back carried all his hurt, all the weariness he felt in no longer being recognised as human by others. 'It's tough being homeless,' he mumbled through the face rest. 'I've got hep C, too. My liver is stuffed.'

And then there was Michael, who was also unused to being touched. He was battling an STD, had rashes all over his body and his kidneys had been failing him. After years of living on the streets, his dream was that his public housing would come through so that he could spend time with his small child, something that being homeless and divorced had made so difficult. He wanted desperately to be a good father, to be someone who could provide again and stand on his own two feet.

These men were men living in the shadows of their previous lives, struggling for the world to see them for the resourceful men they were if just given a second chance. Yet deep inside each of these men was profound trauma, grief and loss. Maybe their story was about coming from a broken home, of being abused, or going in and out of foster care. Maybe they had lost their jobs, or their marriages. Their situations would all vary slightly, but I could reasonably accurately guess at the depth of their emotional damage. Indeed, these men had worked hard over many years learning to harden up, not to show any emotion, and not to communicate their needs. And yet so much of how their lives had fallen apart had its roots in how they were raised as men, in ways that ushered in violence, conflict, crisis and chaos.

For me to have seen these men open up a little and to feel safe through the simple act of hands on flesh with a massage was truly special. It seemed that they knew, or perhaps felt through touch, that they were being seen as a human being, as someone deserving of love, attention and kindness. And they were always so grateful after it too.

We need a seismic change in what we expect of men and how we raise them. I have no desire to be a 'real man', to 'harden up' or to 'man up'. Such language only harms me and all men, as it seeks to co-opt our masculinity into something toxic. Men don't need to be 'real men', we need to be able to talk about our feelings. Men don't need to 'man up', we need to be open to intimacy and learn how to manage conflict in healthy ways. Men don't need to 'harden up', we need to learn to listen better, value consent, never resort to violence or threaten it to get our way with women, ever.

Men who cry, who show vulnerability, who admit they need help and communicate their feelings, or at least try to, are real men as far as I'm concerned. Men who ask for help, don't want to be controlling, do show emotion and simply need a hug are all strong men. We need to encourage men to get help, ask for help and know they won't be shamed or judged for it. This is when vulnerability is strength.

As a society we need to believe in men, we need to end the stigma and refuse to accept long-standing myths about what it is to be a man. We need to raise our boys to know they have a right to boundaries and be safe at all times, and that if they are unfortunate victims of abuse they know they are never to blame.

I know how men suffer in silence. My entire life has been one where I have worked in the company of silently suffering men often paying the price of other men's shaming. It is how men silence each other that troubles me. And it's a very high price to pay. As much as you try to escape expectations as a man, it saturates every space you enter. I myself was a man who for so long was ashamed, clung to my honour and painfully pushed through in silence. I had mistakenly thought my worth as a man was all about *not*

MEN WHO CRY, WHO SHOW VULNERABILITY, WHO ADMIT THEY NEED HELP AND COMMUNICATE THEIR FEELINGS, OR AT LEAST TRY TO, ARE REAL MEN.

asking for help, showing emotion or being vulnerable. But suffering in silence for so many men has resulted in terrible situations and problems, including homelessness, drug addictions, criminal records, poverty, mental ill-health, self-harm, chronic illnesses and permanent disabilities. I have sat in so many big and small rooms with men who have suffered silently, and I ache for you all.

The suicide rate for men in Australia is three times the rate for women. Every day in this country six men die from suicide while another thirty try to take their lives. Clearly our current and long-standing notions of masculinity are doing no one in society any real favours. The crisis of masculinity we're experiencing now is not happening because of the progress of women, feminism or the need for equality, but because we continue to raise our boys on an idea of masculinity that is poisonous to them and all they love, particularly women and children. And it's killing both men and women in record numbers.

The leading cause of preventable death, disability and injury in this country for women aged between eighteen and forty-five is violence from men they know. I often talk to my friends about what they fear most about dating today – for men it's being rejected on a date while for women it's being raped on a date.

No man was born hating women. This is learned behaviour.

Equality is at the heart of all great societies. We can't speak of a prosperous and just society unless women are sitting at the table with men. And by that I mean all women: women of colour, Indigenous women, refugee and immigrant women, trans and queer women, women with disability, young and elderly women, all women. This inequality is an issue for men to correct. A culture that is rife with sexual assault and sexual harassment in the workplace is an issue for men. Rape culture is an issue for men. When women aren't believed when they speak out, that's also an issue for men. When men don't listen to women, that's men holding onto power rather than sharing it. Our outdated patriarchal attitudes have encouraged many women to believe that they are responsible for the abusive behaviours of men. What was she wearing? Why was she out so late? Why did she go back to his place if she wasn't interested? What did she expect after getting drunk? This is rape culture – meaning a culture that blames women for their victimisation – and it remains pervasive.

Sexual harassment, violence against women, child abuse, unequal power, rape culture are all men's issues. All of them. Why? Because we perpetrate most of them, that's why.

When I speak out about male violence against women, it often unleashes so much anger from some men. But why do they feel so angry about making women's lives and safety a priority? How does that hurt them as men? What does that possibly take away from them as men? No one is saying that men's lives don't matter, they do, but the men who lose their lives to violence almost without exception face the same enemy and root cause, which is the violence of men.

So as men, are we willing to relinquish some of our power and privilege? Are we willing to stop reinforcing a culture that allows us to dominate, that allows us always to be believed over women, that allows us to have legitimacy in trying to control the bodies of women, and in being paid more?

What are we willing to give up in the interests of justice and equality as men?

Many men have accused me of being anti-male. I'm not at all. I'm pro-male. I love and believe in men. I believe that our natural state is not one of violence and oppression, that men are taught this and that these lessons can be unlearned. I believe that men *do* want intimacy, to be vulnerable, to be able to express their emotions. I believe that men are losing too, right now, in missing out on the fully realised human beings they can be.

Women have given me strength and inspiration, kindness and compassion throughout my life. My mum and sister are so special to me. They have always been there for me. As I've already said, Nola is my best friend and

A midnight selfie with my sister, Nola, at the end of one of the hundreds of ASRC Wednesday Night Legal Clinics we have done together.

guardian angel. I always feel so safe, heard, loved and cared for by her. She is so incredible and she doesn't even see it.

I care about women living free of male violence not, however, because they are my mum or my sister or my aunt, but because they are *someone*. That is enough. We should care about women because they're human beings not because of their relationship to us as men, because if we do this, no matter how well intentioned we might be, we are simply viewing women as a commodity or possession. Women are fed up with men aiming so low, giving so little, risking almost nothing yet wanting praise and to be made to feel special.

As men we can all be champions for change by taking some really simple action. Here are a few things to get you started on the right road to becoming a better man:

- Believe women. I cannot tell you how vital that is when we live in a rape culture that blames women, silences women and victimises women for speaking up.
- When a woman discloses she is a survivor of abuse or sexual harassment, the simple words of 'I believe you and you are not to blame' are vital, especially when they are uttered by a man. This statement should then be followed by, 'How can I support you to feel safe and to get the help you need?'

- Listen to women and learn from them. I mean really listen to women and hear their struggles, aspirations and challenges, and ask how you can be an ally. Men cannot listen to and learn from women enough right now.
- Don't speak over women. This means not talking over women in public spaces or interrupting them when they are speaking. This may sound small, but when men disregard women in this way women understandably feel dismissed, belittled and silenced.
- Don't 'mansplain' a woman's job to her to tell her what it's like to be a woman - women are the experts at being women. Don't be the guy that, through his actions, says, 'Let my male self-confidence discount your authoritative expertise.'
- Call out rape culture in all its forms. Men rely on the silence (and implicit approval of other men that goes with our silence) to get away with sexist jokes, language and aggressive, controlling behaviour towards women in public. Next time you hear a sexist joke just say, 'Mate, I don't appreciate that and I don't want to hear jokes or comments that put down women, ever.' Or if you are concerned a friend, colleague or family member might be in an abusive relationship, reach

out to the woman (when it's safe for her) and ask if you can help.

- And let's as men reflect on our own language, actions, expectations and behaviour towards the women in our lives. Check our own sense of entitlement. Ask yourself the tough question: Do I feel entitled to a women's time, body, interest, energy, space, finances or attention without her consent? If so, you have much work to do on yourself now. That work is for *you* to do, not for the women in your life to do on your behalf.
- Be a positive role model for your sons, nephews, grandsons, male partners, male colleagues and friends by showing respect to all women in your daily life.

All of these natural courtesies can help start a comprehensive cultural shift in the home, networks and workplace, and help make this a men's issue.

We can understand that no means no and that stop means stop. We can understand that consent is not negotiable – and if you're unsure, ask the woman you're with. She will tell you as long as you're not being threatening or she doesn't fear the situation might escalate into one of violence if she says no.

Isn't it time to say no to outmoded male behaviours and seek to be a 'good man' intead of a 'real man'? Stand up and speak out in support of women's right to live free of sexual harassment and sexual assault, and educate yourself on how you can help end violence against women. Consider becoming a role model or mentor for younger boys, showing them through your words and actions that being a man means respecting women and being mindful of your own behaviour. Take the time to reflect on your own past conduct to see if you might unknowingly be reinforcing sexist attitudes and devaluing the women in your life.

We can all be better men and we deserve to be for our own wellbeing, mental health and self-love. And then such attentiveness will only improve our relationships with all the women in our lives.

12

RESILIENCE, PASSION AND INTEGRITY

So many times I have been in the company of men pushed to the brink of despair.

Once I had a call from a man named Richard, desperate for help with something I knew nothing about. He was in the prime of his life as a man and father, but because of chronic fatigue syndrome he had no life at all, not even the physical strength to play with his children. He was desperate for a remedy and had tried everything from over-the-counter medicines to prescription drugs. He had heard that dehydroepiandrosterone (DHEA), a hormone produced by the adrenal glands and easily available as a tablet from health-food stores in the United States, could be his saviour, but the Therapeutic Goods Administration had banned it in Australia. He wanted to take them on and be the first person here to get access to it. I had no idea how we would possibly do that, but his voice was so full of a desperation I will never forget that I said, 'Yes, let's try.' We found a major law firm to join in, took on the Australian government and we bloody won! And Richard gave me a bullet after our victory.

I still have this bullet, but don't really know what to do with it, or how to feel about having the bullet he was going to use to take his own life. He had it plated and made into a keychain, and gave it to me. As he handed it to me, he admitted his original intention for it, adding, 'I'd kept it for so long to do this until I met you. I finally have my life back, Kon, and now I want to give this to you.'

Another time, some years ago, I was sitting in one of our cramped, lemon-coloured intake rooms with a refugee. 'I want to go back inside. Let me go back,' Yazdan said. 'I don't know how to survive out here after five and a half years inside a cage. I know no other world in Australia.'

Yazdan was begging me to get him put back in Baxter Detention Centre from where he'd just been released. He'd been brought to the ASRC by a deeply concerned friend who was hoping I could convince him not to go back. We'd spoken for several hours and I'd explained just how we could support him in starting a new life, that it was normal to be afraid, that he was what is called 'institutionalised' after being locked up for so long in such horrendous conditions. By the end of it I was begging him not to go back inside. Unfortunately, nothing I said worked. The next day he flew back to South Australia, went to the front gate of the detention centre and asked to be let back in. Thankfully, they said no.

Dig deep to find your true resilience; it's remarkable how useful it can be. Too often we see our struggles as personal deficiencies, as something we feel we have to lock away. It's so important that you remind yourself that – despite all of your struggles, baggage, self-doubt, fear and anxiety – you have survived. Despite at times feeling unable to get out of bed and face the world, you're still here, still going, fighting and using every ounce of your energy to appear normal. This is resilience. Your ability to survive and thrive against the odds is your resilience. It's your emotional power bank.

When we were children, most of us also had another attribute in abundance: empathy. A child sees a person for who they are. A child doesn't see the quality of someone's clothes, and doesn't yet know about stereotypes, or about fear. Children grow up with empathy and then we teach them to see these other things, so they too become cynical adults. Empathy for yourself and others matters because it's grounded in seeing the other much more inclusively – not just as the other but as you, me, each other. It's about rising above our own self-interest and becoming something better.

Resilience, empathy and passion make a powerful combination, and yet many people feel that these qualities should be tempered in people – that people who possess them can be too earnest, too committed. My passion is the one quality I have that has drawn the greatest scorn and judgment from others. When I was twenty-two and still studying Social Work, my placement supervisor said to the organisation where I was doing my on-the-job training, and in front of me, 'If he can just get rid of that fire in the belly, Kon will be fine.' I will never forget those words. At the time they stung so hard. To be told that I was too passionate, felt too much, cared too much, was too much of an idealist was just awful. How was being idealistic a problem, a weakness that I had to stamp out of me? It's so strange that we live in a time where the best in us – idealism, passion, curiosity, critical thinking and community organising – is often damned, and the worst in us – racism, fear, intolerance, prejudice and individualism – so often inflamed.

It seems to me that those people who tell you what you can't do, can't be, do it largely because they don't want to be reminded of those things they've already abandoned in order to fit in. And I'm saying right now that fitting in is overrated. If we follow the dull drum of conformity, it will be regret that wakes us each day rather than the passion and excitement of what we can be or are striving to discover to

ONLY
THE PASSIONATE
CAN CHANGE
THE WORLD AND
TRANSFORM IT.

be. Only the passionate can change the world and transform it. Passion means so much to me that I even have the word tattooed in Greek on my right arm. It's there to remind me always to do everything with passion. Beware the dream crushers, of people with missing or hollow hearts. Beware people who tell you you're a bleeding heart – I would rather run red and bleed than not beat at all. Beware people whose life slogans are in reality 'DO NOTHING'.

It's true that my passion and beliefs have got me into real trouble. I once had a job helping people with disabilities, which was a responsibility I took seriously, but the management had taken issue with some of my advocacy. 'You need to remember whose side you're on, Kon. We're on the same team. I want to give you another chance, but you can't accuse staff of discrimination and breaking the law.' I'd been warned. Of course I didn't want to get fired, but these people needed someone to speak up on their behalf. So I made it clear that I would continue to do what I'd been doing, which was to protect the human rights of the people I'd been employed to. And that was it, I was gone a week later. My manager handed me an envelope without saying a word. I was given until the end of the day to pack up my things and paid two weeks' notice.

I'm sure none of us wants to lose our job, but I think what's far worse is to lose yourself, lose your values, lose your principles and what you stand for. Most of us can find another job, but you can't get back your soul or your values. They are yours and they are precious. No one owns you – you own yourself and the choices you ultimately make.

For me, integrity means doing what is moral and right even when there is no immediate payoff, even if no one is watching, even when it's not convenient or easy. Integrity means holding your ground even when there's a cost to you because it's the right thing to do. There is nothing worse than not being able to look at yourself in the mirror, to be someone who struggles to live with the decisions they have made. The person who is self-aware and knows where the line is that they will not cross is a powerful person.

To be neutral in times of injustice is to be complicit with it. Indeed, Desmond Tutu once said, 'If you are neutral in situations of injustice, you have chosen the side of the oppressor.' Neutrality is for those lucky enough to engage in debates around human rights as abstract conversations rather than real life-and-death challenges. If we choose not to protest, choose not to speak out, we're more than just a bystander, we're an enabler. Oppression thrives on our collective silence, apathy or indifference, but it cannot prosper when we refuse to cooperate.

But remember, you're not standing up for your principles or values if you only do so when it pertains to you – that's not principles in action, that's just self-interest.

Interestingly, the same university that had fired me in 1999 many years later made me the face of their summer campaign, their Alumni of the Year, and I was splashed across Melbourne trams and on television ads as a reason to study there. In the interests of full disclosure, I had, in fact, been sacked from every paid job I had before the ASRC and nearly every place that sacked me has, years later, given me a prestigious award in recognition of my commitment to human rights or as an alumnus. I'm actually okay with this because it means more positive publicity for the ASRC and the opportunity to create even more awareness of the problems facing refugees, which can only be a good thing. Also, the people who were responsible are long gone. The truth is I'm actually very proud of the universities where I've worked and studied, and they now genuinely welcome people seeking asylum and have become great allies. I would have missed these new working relationships if I'd let my hurt feelings and ego get in the way of what was best for refugees.

So there's some satisfaction there for me now, but I won't lie, at the time getting sacked was humiliating. I felt I had let my family down and was yet again unemployed. The satisfaction now comes from knowing that I held onto my values and who I was, even during those thankless times, and that my integrity helped protect me. And the reason I'm sure of this is that every time I got sacked I went on to an even better job, without fail. I'm convinced that standing by your values makes you unbreakable, because someone can only take them from you if you let them. Jobs come and go – and I don't mean to be flippant here because I know people have mortgages and family responsibilities – but your values, what you stand for, the line you draw, these are the essence of you. And once you start compromising, you start to lose your moral compass and slowly, little by little, you also start to lose respect and pride in the person you are or want to be for you, your family, your community and your friends.

The first paid professional job I ever had was working part time at a homeless centre. One day it was close to dinnertime, during which more than two hundred homeless men would be fed, and it had started raining. The queue of hungry and homeless men waiting to eat stretched almost around the entire block. I thought it just wasn't right to leave these men outside as the rain strengthened. I approached my manager and asked if we could let the men in to be seated. 'The clothes on their back might be all they have, and soon they'll be soaking wet,' I remember saying. 'That doesn't seem right.' Then I offered to serve dinner to each of the men myself. My manager was far from impressed with my impertinence and told me that wasn't how things were done there, and that the men would have to wait outside. I tried again, saying

I was happy to do whatever was needed to get them out of the rain and fed. That was the last day I worked there. I was seen as a troublemaker, someone who didn't know how to toe the line. But how could I have said nothing and just watched the men wet and cold, possibly in their only clothes, queuing for a hot meal?

I think our integrity is most tested when people betray us and try to drag us down to their level. Ensuring this doesn't happen, though, is easier said than done. I'm sure we've all been let down, hurt and betrayed by others. It hurts and makes it difficult to trust people again. When it happens to me I remind myself that the greatest power I can give away in such moments is the power of who I am, what I stand for, what my values are. The minute I allow these to be influenced or shaped by someone else, I've not only betrayed myself but also given this surprise foe a power over me that they could only dream of. 'See, they are just like the rest of them,' I can hear them thinking. 'See, they are no better than us.'

No matter how tempting in the heat of the moment it might be to retaliate, once you go down that path, it's the point of no return. Don't give up your integrity, your values and what you stand for in a moment of anger and hurt. It doesn't matter if it's justified and warranted, when they go low you must always go high because that's what matters. You're now called on to be the bigger person and not defend yourself, because to do so is putting you before everyone else. It can be painful, it's certainly not easy or convenient, but I promise you that in the long term you will be better off. Remember, we live in a country where the tall poppy syndrome does exist, where sadly a minority of people want to see you fail and fall, and will take glee in it. Always rise above it; that's what you deserve. Never lose your values and who you are; that's what living your values means.

13

THE FACTS

It's time now to take a look at Australia's bigger picture and see how things currently stand. I'm warning you now, it's not pretty. And no wonder we feel disheartened about our politics when we consider just what's going on.

We're a country that has allocated billions to fight wars on terror but only crumbs to fight the war on male violence against women, which has taken more than seven hundred lives over the past decade alone. We can send troops to the far reaches of Afghanistan, but nine out of ten women escaping an abusive male partner cannot find a safe bed for the night because our federal government continues to cut services for them. White ribbons on the lapels of our male political leaders do not bring back dead women. Don't women deserve better?

We can offer massive tax breaks to mining companies but can't afford a living wage. We're a country that would rather drug test the poor than help them, sending them into the arms of shame, isolation and exclusion. Single mothers are now forced to have a third party verify their relationship status to receive income support, a reminder that women's voices and word are never enough. The homeless are spoken of as an inconvenience, as an eyesore, but tent cities spring up in our city centres when no solid ground can be found to give root to the foundations of hope and a future. We are a country that banishes those who seek our protection to hellholes on Nauru or Manus to die. We have politicians who highlight what it costs us in tax to care for the elderly, disabled and poor (as though these are bad things) but then hide the cost of negative gearing, tax avoidance by multinationals, and offshore prisons.

In Australia today 40 per cent of the workforce is in insecure employment and one out of ten immigrants are here on temporary visas. This precarious labour force, combined with wage theft and privatisation, means that trickle-down economics is more of a myth now than ever. Indeed, profits for corporations are up 20 per cent while wages have increased by just 2 per cent. And to add insult to injury, 678 of Australia's biggest corporations don't pay any tax in Australia, while funding for education, health and welfare continues to shrink.

We have become a country that wants 24/7 service on 9 to 5 wages.

I work alongside kids who are growing up in families where neither parent can work. We have a government in power that wants to imprison ten-year-old children without charge for two weeks, and now we're being told to fear Australian African youths. We've learned to weaponise, criminalise and demonise brown and black bodies – and it's only black and brown people whom we speak of as gangs, not young white people.

There is no doubt that political and moral issues are viewed very differently by the politicians themselves and that, it seems, at every turn the politically expedient decision will win out.

We have made the monstrous and evil the mundane and the everyday. We have taken the unspeakable and obscene and used twisted tongues to reshape it into our national interest.

And things are now at the point where we can no longer just blame the politicians. We get the leadership we deserve. What needs to happen now is for us to become active and to show the way. It needs to start with us. And not because it's our fault, but because things can't change unless we actively bend the arc of justice back to us as a community.

We live in times where people ask us to justify being a loving and caring person who has empathy for others. Compassion at its most basic is putting yourself in the shoes of another person and wanting them to be treated how you would want to be. It's simple moral accountability. We have allowed cynicism and apathy to get a hold of our moral imagination; we have been beaten down for caring by being called bleeding hearts. We've been ridiculed in our communities for championing social justice, told that we're social justice warriors, as though being a warrior for justice is a bad thing. I can think of nothing more honourable.

There can be another Australia for us, one of hope, inclusion, compassion, belonging, prosperity and welcome. We want and need generational and systemic change, but if we want a better world we have to fight for it, not just scrap for small wins. The personal is always deeply political because the decisions of our political leaders have real consequences for us. The personal is deeply political because if we don't give our anger and despair a fitting name, and a social, economic and political context that includes other marginalised people, then we have the politics of division and fear that will triumph over us.

We need to be an inclusive and fair country. So what do we need to become one?

We need to challenge our privilege, show that civil rights matter and fight for the change that we want. We need to speak not just about human rights but also of civil, social, economic and political rights, which are at the heart of equality and equity. A movement grounded in

THERE CAN
BE ANOTHER
AUSTRALIA
FOR US, ONE OF
HOPE, INCLUSION,
COMPASSION,
BELONGING,
PROSPERITY AND
WELCOME.

this knows that without economic self-determination and participation, we have nothing; if we're excluded from the economy, we're also excluded from participating in society. We need to be fearless, to lead with our moral imagination and passion and to build our independence.

We need money to go into social housing instead of detention centres and prisons.

We need a holistic long-term model of care for people with mental health, drug and alcohol issues.

We need to raise a new generation of men, and we need strength-based models of early intervention care. Imagine an Australia where the only gap we speak of is for young people on a gap year, and where the family home is the safest place for a woman to be. Inclusion, prosperity, equality and freedom, these are the foundations that will build a great and thriving Australia. How are we going to get there? What needs to change in how we lead our collective lives?

It seems that the more stuff we have, the less we seem to appreciate it. But strangely we still want more of it and so we keep buying more and more stuff, trying to fill a spiritual hole. Clearly it doesn't work, and it makes sense that it doesn't. Trying to find meaning, faith and purpose in our lives through acquiring things seems like a staggering waste of money and energy. And that heedless consumption also stops us from connecting to our true selves, our hearts and our relationships. Martin Luther King wrote, 'Our hope for creative living … lies in our ability to re-establish the moral ends of our lives in personal character and social justice.'

Every time someone tries to quash my passion, telling me I'm a bleeding heart or that I'm too naive or idealistic, or that the issues are more complex than I understand them to be and that we need to be this cruel to refugees, the poor, the disabled and First Nations people for their own sake, I now say to them: 'Enough.'

I will not justify my decency, my conscience, my resistance, my opposition, my rage, my disgust any longer. I am not the problem. I am not the enemy. Nor are the people I stand with and for. I will not be silent, I will not be complicit, I will not accept this as the new normal.

It's time for real ideas, movements owned by the people for the people. It's time for an uprising against the politics of division, hate, fear-mongering and individualism. Of the politics of greed at all costs, power at all costs, and a society built on the fiction of lifters and leaners.

It's time to listen to women. For too long they have been left to do too much of the work. Now it's their time to be heard, to be believed, to have equal pay, representation, sexual-harassment-free workplaces, adequate child care, access to the contraception they need, the right to control their body, the right to feel safe in their own family home or the streets any time of the day or night.

It's time for us to listen to the vision of First Nations people for our shared country on how we can create restorative justice. It's time for political narratives woven with our stories, with our shared hopes, aspirations, struggles and dreams at the centre. It's time for a discussion on the issues and ideas that can transform our lives, change a generation and end generational inequality being passed on and on.

Let's talk about a Bill of Rights, a treaty, a living wage. Let's talk about social housing investment that could end homelessness in a generation; affordable higher education; a future of work that leaves no part of our community behind; a zero-tolerance culture in every workplace, community space and household when it comes to sexual harassment and male violence against women; leadership that frames the plight of refugees as the humanitarian issue that it is; investment in renewable energy that enables us to have real emission targets that give us real action on climate change; real pathways and support for people with disabilities to thrive not just survive; investment in Indigenous-controlled and -operated solutions to end generational theft, exclusion and prejudice that stops the gap from being closed.

I want an optimism again for our country. We all do. We're hungry for change.

I dream of my red ochre country, with its boundless plains to share, being a home of welcome, where the arms of equality embrace us all. Where fear and bigotry find no quarter or place to breathe.

Yet we are constantly being told by our political leaders that change must wait. They insist that it is not the time to Bring Them Here, to act on climate change, for a treaty, or for action on male violence against women. The same stalling tactics were employed around the issue of marriage equality. Think of how long the LGBTIQA community had to wait for the right to marry, as though the recognition of same-sex relationships would somehow diminish those between a man and a woman; and, similarly, that a treaty would somehow erase white privilege, or that welcoming refugees would somehow impinge on the freedom of others.

Well, I am here to tell you: the time for change is NOW. No more waiting; no more excuses.

Greed and individualism do not build prosperous or connected communities. Hate and anger do not nurture perspective and patience, they just tear us all down in the end. Cowardice inspires only a retreat from our best selves, and hubris does not make great leaders.

The world is an unjust place because of the inaction of good people, people who say not my issue, not my problem, not my backyard. We need to have much more kindness and forgiveness for the fact that people make mistakes, they might develop addictions to deal with their pain and trauma, or become homeless and destitute, disconnected from their communities, their bodies, their selves. No one wants to be a burden, a problem, an issue, a target for people's rage, anger and bitterness. And by that I'm not saying that people aren't accountable for their actions or that they're perpetual victims; of course people have agency and choices and need to be held responsible, but it is not always that easy or clear-cut. It assumes that there is an even playing field for all, that there is an equity and equality of opportunity to contribute, participate and succeed. The truth is there is not.

Courage is contagious and the more good we do, the more people will want to follow our example. We all want to be part of something good, positive and constructive, something that makes things better. We all want to know that we matter. We all want to be heard. We all want to love and to know that we're loved. We want to be seen, valued, part of a community, part of something deeper and greater than us. None of us signs up by choice to a life not fully lived.

Life is so precious and short, and it deserves the best of you – *you* deserve the best of you, so live with passion, enthusiasm and excitement in all that you do. Be your best self, do things that scare and inspire you, do things that make you think.

And in spite of these challenging times, there is good news and hope everywhere. Just recently marriage equality was realised, there is still conjecture whether or not the Adani coalmine will go ahead, attempts to send 410 refugees in Australia back to Manus and Nauru have been thwarted, and recently we saw the first Indigenous woman elected to the Victorian parliament. Women across the country have spoken out publicly against their sexual abuse in the workplace as part of the #MeToo movement. First Nations people from every corner of Australia came together to craft and commit to the extraordinary Uluru Statement. All attempts to scrap 18C of the Racial Discrimination Act that would have allowed unfettered hate speech were defeated by every multicultural community fighting against it. And the planned draconian changes to the Citizenship Act failed as well, because of our power.

I remain hopeful about our future because the Australia we can be is found in the hearts of the young and old who demand it be kinder and fairer. I remain hopeful because more and more Australians want to be on the right side of history, something that we saw with marriage equality in spite of all the attempts to stop love and fairness from carrying the day.

There are good stories to be told everywhere. Just imagine if our twenty-four-hour news cycle focused its energy on spotlighting stories of our collective kindness for the greater good. Imagine if the leading stories were about the personal joy that marriage equality had brought to the LGBTIQA community, or about the refugees who are reviving our rural and regional communities through agriculture, or of the soup kitchens for the homeless run by local Sikh communities, or of our Indigenous elders taking young men back to country to connect to sixty thousand years of culture and to heal. If our senses were overwhelmed each day by acts of kindness, change and hope, we would be a different country, a far more equal, loving and welcoming community.

Our stories of hope and compassion can also be seen in so many of our charities. They are there in our Rotary and Lions clubs, and Rural Australians for Refugees, which welcomes refugees into country towns. They can be seen each week in the parents who give up their weekends to coach the local footy or soccer teams, and the thousands who volunteer in community legal centres across our land to ensure everyone has access to justice.

Stories of communities are also found in our not-for-profit radio stations, community gardens and lifesaving clubs. They are in our IT communities, which conduct hackathons to find ways technology can solve thorny humanitarian puzzles and challenges. They are in our young entrepreneurs, who start up social enterprises to provide pathways and employment opportunities for people who are disadvantaged. They are in the hundreds of thousands of Australians who join fundraisers such as Run 4 Refugees, the Royal Children's Hospital Appeal or Movember. They include the nurses and doctors of our overstretched public hospitals, our ambulance workers and firefighters. The good news stories are in our primary schools, volunteer-run breakfast programs, our scout and girl guide groups, and in our scientists who tirelessly search for medical breakthroughs and cures. Everywhere you look you can see the power of hope.

14

THE POWER OF FAILURE

A TV producer at the ABC thought I could be an actor after seeing my stand-up and asked me to audition for the show *The Librarians*. I was meant to be a Lothario and charm a young woman, but the audition was an absolute disaster. I was as sexy as a can of baked beans (the kind that comes with bacon), and the more I tried to ooze seductive machismo, the more stiff and nervous I became. Each time I leaned in with a line, I wanted to throw up. Thankfully that didn't happen, but it went so badly I never heard from them again, not even a phone call. My television career was over before it started.

Admittedly there wasn't too much at stake with that audition, but fear of failure can be an emotional and psychological bogeyman that can take charge of so many of our lives. Fear of failing at something can paralyse the greatest imaginations, aspirations and dreams.

So take a moment to consider that if we own our failures with perspective, patience, forgiveness, reflection and kindness, we open ourselves up to the most incredible opportunities for growth, development and success. How can we ever truly fail if we're just honouring ourselves, our journey, our voices and trying to live an authentic life? The short answer is that we cannot.

I have lost my way and fallen apart so many times. I've rolled myself up into a ball of despair and played the victim to my life circumstances. I have disappointed people and let them down. People who looked up to me have felt neglected by me and not a priority for me, and I have lost dear friendships from it.

I have let ego and pride get the best of me at times by wanting to be right, wanting to hide that I might be unsure of myself at times. Throughout my twenties I was scared and small, unwilling to take any risks and open my heart. I wasted years of my life to fear.

I have tried to be perfect, someone who always does the right thing, the thoughtful thing. In retrospect, though, that was more about being in control than allowing myself to be vulnerable. That was when I wouldn't allow myself to be messy and human, when I was hiding behind work rather than putting my heart out there.

Failure has taught me that you need to let people make their own choices and have their own agency. No one really appreciates you for doing what you thought was best for them; you can only own what you want for yourself and nothing more.

In the past I was too slow and took too long to tell the people I loved how I felt, and when that chance passed forever my heart was crushed with it. I bottled up my needs and feelings, scared that they weren't worthwhile and would find no acceptance.

As you now know, I have regrets, too. I wish I'd spent far more time with my father and shown him more love, patience and kindness when he was alive. That is my greatest regret and it leaves a daily ache in me. That is my one failure I can't forgive myself for.

My employment failures are numerous. I've already said this once, but before starting the ASRC I had been sacked from every job I had. Actually, I really do think that's worth repeating. I had been sacked from *every* single paid job I had. As it turned out, it all became a blessing. Another failure that stung for a long time was not getting into law after high school the first time. But I got there in the end.

I'm now in my forties and still yet to start a family. As you know, I had my first intimate relationship when I was thirty-two, and the long wait had left me feeling so inadequate, as if I'd been playing an impossible game of catch-up. In fact my first couple of relationships were terribly confronting, because although I was in my thirties

I was so inexperienced with that level of intimacy. I struggled and had to work hard to be present and to be vulnerable. All of my exes are wonderful women, and I am so grateful to have shared my life with each of them. These six relationships have shown me ways to grow and change and become the man that I am today, in particular, my last relationship and partner, with whom I shared my life for six years. I will be forever indebted to her for all she taught me about compassion, love, vulnerability, intimacy, self - love and how I need to grow and evolve to be the best person I can be, to my partner and myself. And, of course, I am still growing.

I yearn to be a father but so far that hasn't happened for me. I observe my friends and relatives with their own children. It's hard not to feel envious and even a little resentful at times, because it seems that parenthood just happened for them. I know it's much easier for a man than a woman in her forties dealing with this, but that doesn't mean it's easy. It may be too late for me, though I really believe I'd make a great father. On thinking about the patience, life experience and love I could give a child, I try to stay open to possibilities and keep a positive perspective.

I've already shared that I was bullied through most of primary school and that at high school I used to hide in the library, and that past high school teachers told me to drop out because I would amount to nothing. And I had no friends at university. All of those formative years of failing helped shape me and make me even more resilient.

And you've seen that I have battled with weight issues my entire life. Comfort eating has been a real problem for me and I've often turned to food to help me cope with loneliness and feeling unlovable. Generally speaking, women have said no to me far more often than yes when I've asked them out. At times I still struggle with low self-esteem, and more often than not I'm still really shy and awkward in any new social setting, especially around women.

In the past I have truly sucked at striking a work–life balance, and my artistic efforts were all a flaming hot mess.

And there is not a week that goes by at the ASRC where I don't feel like I'm failing, that whatever I do isn't good enough, that I'm disappointing people. At times I still feel like an impostor. I often wonder when I'm at my lowest whether I have actually made any real difference for people, and I always wish I was doing more, helping more in changing things for refugees.

Both of my parents felt like failures. My dad's most often repeated story to me was of how he was pulled out of school at nine and how that ended his dreams of becoming a lawyer or a doctor, and my mother never got to make the choices she wanted for herself either – everything was pre-determined by poverty, necessity and compromise. To me,

THE POWER OF FAILURE IS THAT IT'S ALWAYS BRINGING US CLOSER TO THE PERSON WE'RE MEANT TO BE AND THE LIFE WE'RE MEANT TO LIVE.

though, my parents are the two greatest successes I have ever met. All of their so-called failures were in fact selfless sacrifices that enabled my sister and I to thrive and succeed. What a gift they gave to me. Both of them abandoned their dreams, and the lives and happiness they deserved, so that their struggle would not be the legacy they passed on to us.

I share all of this because failure contains the power to humble and humanise us. It can teach us to be gracious, to have perspective and not to lose hope in ourselves. It can help us learn that we are fragile, that we fuck up, are scared, are flawed, can be petty, can wish ill for others, can be jealous, angry, bitter, small and shallow at times. We are all these things. There is no perfect, just a continuum of messiness that makes us human and beautiful.

Contrary to what some might think, failure doesn't weaken us, and it shouldn't leave us feeling ashamed because we tried something and it didn't work out. The power of failure is that it's always bringing us closer to the person we're meant to be and the life we're meant to live.

Martin Luther King puts it so eloquently when he writes, 'Shattered dreams are a hallmark of our mortal life.' In other words, failure is inescapable, but much more than that, failure is part of living a good life.

We can't have intimacy without failure, and we can't have love without failure. To live an authentic life, we must accept our needs, desires and moments of darkness in their entirety. We cannot censor our true selves for short-term acceptance by others; this will not make us happy.

What if I don't know the answer? What if I make a mistake? What if I lose face, make a fool of myself and embarrass myself? What if people see me as an impostor, as someone who doesn't deserve to be here right now? We all have a soundtrack that keeps playing in our heads telling us at all times that we can't afford to fail, that the price is too high. The truth is, though, that in not taking action, in not taking risks, we have already paid the highest price. That price is our own happiness.

When we fail, we grow. When we fail, we learn. When we fail, we are alive as we have followed our heart, our curiosity and taken a risk, an investment in our self-worth. Failure is an act of self-love because we only feel that we've failed when we've lost or not achieved something that matters to us.

Ask yourself when your last significant experience of emotional growth was. And following that, ask yourself when you last truly emotionally reflected, found more depth to yourself and challenged yourself while in safety and comfort. Ask yourself how many of your best life experiences (whether to do with work, intimate relationships, travel, creative explorations or new friendships) occurred during moments of safety and no risk. I'm sure you only need one hand at most to count them, if at all.

Many of my best qualities, instilled by my parents, have all been strengthened through failure. My ability to be in the moment with people, to be vulnerable, hold a public space when I'm talking with authenticity comes from my suffering. To have suffered in so many ways and to have experienced grief in so many forms has built great resilience in me. Now at the heart of me I feel that I can get through anything. That no matter how small or scared I feel inside, I can roar with confidence and lead and inspire. This is because I feel it all so deeply; it's so personal to me. In fact, the more vulnerable, shy and out of my depth I'm feeling, the more I'm able to draw on this reserve of fearlessness – and protection – that I have inside of me. And this deep centre has in large part been forged from failure.

15

WHAT PRICE FREEDOM?

It was an evening in November 2017 and they had cut the boat's motor. We were told not to make any noise because to do so risked the Papua New Guinea Navy spotting and arresting us. We heard the sound of well-worn paddles cutting through the dark-blue waters and the splashing of fish keeping time with us.

The irony was not lost on me: I was in the hands of a people smuggler. But more than that, I was going to visit men stuck where they were because they had once clambered into the boat of a people smuggler.

The vessel itself looked nothing at all like how it had been described to me. It was small, rickety and felt really unstable, as if my weight alone could cause it to capsize if I didn't stay still. It wasn't at all what had been promised to us. And, just like so many people seeking asylum had done, I had to trust what the fixer had told me. I had to trust him because there was no other way to get to my destination. An overland crossing was not an option; the only 'safe passage' was by sea.

Do the circumstances of this story so far sound a little familiar? The way people might trust the hollow promises of a people smuggler? And of travelling over water because there was no other option? The major difference here, of course, was that my life was not in danger.

In spite of its flimsy and worn appearance, this boat and others like it, also belonging to people smugglers, had, for the previous four weeks, been 'vessels of hope'. Some boats had smuggled in food and water to keep the men alive, other boats smuggled in journalists who would in turn tell these men's stories to a national and global audience, and boats smuggled in people like me, who were there to advocate for the men's freedom. I couldn't help but think how damning it was and is that non-refugees needed to bear witness and report back before the refugees themselves would be believed.

The forty-five minutes at sea felt like a long time. It made me reflect on those courageous people who had undertaken journeys of forty-five hours or even forty-five days, and how they had to trust in the sea and in their leaky boat to get them safely to land.

We passed the main checkpoint in complete silence.

Jana Favero (ASRC Director of Advocacy and Campaigns), Natasha Blucher (ASRC Detention Advocacy

Manager) and I weren't scared of getting arrested and deported; we had accepted those risks when we'd made the decision to do this. Our only worry was in failing the men on Manus Island. For us to have come so far now, only to break our promise to them, would have been devastating.

We huddled in the little boat waiting for a sign to land. Then, as promised, there were men on shore who signalled to us using torches and lights from their phones. They were our lighthouse and guided us in, helping us to land safely.

I stepped onto the sand and almost lost my footing, disorientated by anticipation and uncertainty as well as by the sheer adrenaline at having made it. But all of that was short-lived and taken over by the astonishing power of the heat. It was so overwhelming, I felt the energy just drain from my body. We caught our breath briefly before around ten men wrapped their arms around us, as if we were family or old friends. Almost immediately I felt safe and at home. These men would stay by our sides for the next five hours. They guided us, took us to see the sickest men, made us tea, kept us safe. Five brave men in particular – Abdul Aziz Adam, Behrouz Boochani, Ezatullah Kakar, Walid Zazai and Benham Satah – had been extraordinary leaders and heroes, and were unwaveringly committed to making sure all the men incarcerated on Manus could be safe and one day free.

We started walking in the direction of the centre, but nothing could have prepared me for what I saw. All the lies our politicians had told us about Manus died in an instant when I saw it for myself. It was so much worse than anything you have read or been told. The only way I can think to describe it is that it was a living graveyard. This was a place where my country had decided to leave more than 400 human beings to die.

This regional processing centre had been built to destroy hope, to kill dreams, to erase any memory people had that they were once human. It was a place built on the dead spirits of freedom seekers and the corpses of men who came seeking our protection. This was where Reza Barati had lived, where Hamed Shamshiripour and Faysal Ahmed had slept. Our guides' voices dropped to a hush as they pointed out places of mourning and grief everywhere we walked.

It was so dark, so vast, so brutal in its architecture. Every space had been organised to criminalise, humiliate and degrade the men. The centre itself was surrounded by high steel fences, metres high, that were topped with multiple strands of razor wire. But, as Behrouz would say to me later that night, 'Kon, it's not the walls, barbed-wire fences or the cruelty of this place that destroys us. It's being separated from hope, from safety, from family and freedom.'

Manus was a prison that had suffocated these men's freedoms to such a point that they could no longer dream. Indeed, one man confessed that exact thing to me with his words, 'Even my dreams cannot escape this place.' And clearly these men, who had been through so much, were all trapped in a waking nightmare.

Once we were guided inside the complex, through the tall gates, I was quickly struck by the physical appearance of the men. So many of them had arrived on Manus on the cusp of manhood at nineteen or twenty, but now, only several years later, they had the bent and scarred bodies of old men, and all because of our constant neglect and abuse. I asked them what life was like for them. 'We don't live,' they told me. 'We just exist. And we wait and wait and wait.'

The centre itself resembled the footage you've likely seen for Guantanamo Bay – a hellhole built on top of a beach paradise. I stopped for a moment to think about this. Those men had spent nearly five years looking out to the beach and sea, which were only metres away, but they had never been able to walk on the sand or go for a swim. They were reduced to staring and wondering, or perhaps to thinking of their own boat journeys and those people they knew who had perished on the way.

They showed me where they had queued for up to three hours for their medicines. It was along a narrow corridor that at its end had a counter behind glass, rather like a bank, with a few narrow openings to pass the men their pills and other medication. They showed me the soccer field, which had been fashioned from hard rocks, stones and dirt. It wasn't fit to walk on, let alone to play the world game on. Then the men explained that how, until just recently, the centre had been segregated, with half of the men forbidden to mix or speak with the other half. Effectively there had been two prisons within the complex. The men had been arbitrarily separated by a Berlin Wall–like barbed-wire fence. There was no reason given by the authorities for doing this; they did it just because they could. This was a place where logic and reason didn't seem to exist.

I was shown flimsy tin structures that looked like small abandoned aeroplane hangars and told how hundreds of people used to sleep in there in bunks. I tried to picture crowds of men piled in on top of each other to the point of near suffocation, with just a few feeble fans to battle the brutal heat. Now, though, I saw that the men slept on the tops of shipping containers, using the height as a means of protection from being attacked by the locals.

I saw men lifting buckets of contaminated water out of wells that they had been forced to dig to stay alive. Our government had ordered that their water be cut off. Let me repeat that – the Australian government had ordered that more than four hundred men be cut off from any water source. The men now bathed in green wheelie bins, and many of them were covered in angry red rashes, with infections and sores on their backs and legs, and in their eyes and ears. I saw men with swollen and purple feet from stepping on filthy nails. I saw a man have an epileptic fit with no medicine to counter it; and I saw another man bedridden, also without any medication for his diabetes and kidney condition. This was a humanitarian catastrophe.

Whatever you have read about the conditions on Manus Island, you need to know it was far worse and the places that these men have now been moved on to are simply smaller prisons. Nothing has improved for the men still there after an agonisingly slow five years.

Yet amid all this horror that I was seeing with my own eyes, something truly extraordinary was happening. These men, who had been robbed of everything, still showed decency, compassion and love for us. It was a profound truth of the enduring and indestructible nature of our humanity.

On the night we were there, the men insisted on making us some tea and sharing what little food they had. They wouldn't take no for an answer – hospitality and welcoming strangers was in their blood. I remember thinking, These are the sort of men our country needs. So we sat on the floor of a shipping container sipping tea and eating biscuits like family, like we were brothers and sisters with the men on Manus. We joked, took selfies and talked about our dreams, aspirations and futures as if we were in another place and time.

I was so humbled by the courage and generosity of these men. The government had banked on all the men turning on one another once water, food, electricity and medicine were cut, yet these men did not sink to the government's level. In what can only be described as the direst of circumstances, they had found a way to work together, rationing what little food had been smuggled in, sharing medicines, digging wells together and providing comfort to one another for an entire month before being brutally removed under the threat of violence.

What I hadn't understood until I visited this hellhole of a prison was that for the last four and a half years it was the only place in all of Papua New Guinea where the asylum seekers felt any sense of agency, self-determination and safety. After being discarded by the Turnbull government, the men themselves now ran what was once their prison. At last they could move freely among one another, and they would be the ones to decide how the small stores of food, medicine and water would be shared – and shared with kindness rather than having to queue three hours for a tablet. For a brief time they were men again. They were men with choices, no matter how small; they were men with dignity, no matter how compromised. So it's hardly surprising that they did everything they possibly could to stay in there. I will never forget leaving the ruined centre and turning back to watch the men wrap huge chains around the gate and lock them tight to keep themselves safe.

Although my visit to Manus was brief, it profoundly affected me. I was, in fact, so broken by it that the following week I burst into tears every time I spoke of it. Some people worried that I was completely fried, while others were concerned that I might have contracted malaria while there. I hadn't. The truth is my experience was absolutely nothing compared to that of so many others, many of whom paid the ultimate price for our government's cruelty. Reza Barati paid too heavy a price, beaten to death at the age of twenty-three on Manus; so too did Omid Masoumali when he set himself on fire on Nauru to end his unbearable suffering, at twenty-four. Faysal Ishak Ahmed, twenty-seven, and Hamid Khazaei, twenty-four, both died from medical neglect, Hamid from what began as a simple cut foot. It's absolutely shameful to think that for four years, from 2013 to 2017, more refugees died on Manus Island and Nauru than were safely resettled by Australia.

It's heartbreaking to acknowledge that we have largely become desensitised to the horror, to the deaths, to the waste of human potential, to the abrogation of the rule of law and human rights affecting people seeking asylum. It's time to acknowledge that the debate that has controlled the public's imagination on refugees for the last twenty years has been a fictitious one. And it's time to change that.

Through the ASRC's Innovation Hub, more than one thousand people have successfully graduated from TAFE and dozens have started their own small businesses. Young people who arrived by boat without a word of English are now studying double degrees at university, and more than half of all the paid professional roles in our Innovation Hub are now held by people from refugee backgrounds.

At last the real and long overdue change in the movement and the debate is starting to be led by refugees themselves, as it should be. Change is being guided by their struggles, lived experiences and voices. Most significantly, refugees have always resisted with their bodies, spirits and courage. Today more than eighteen hundred refugees continue to bravely protest and fight for their freedom on Manus and Nauru. And in the Australian community more than twenty-five thousand people are fighting for their freedom under a new draconian legal system with no true access to justice or a safety net.

The refugees I meet at the ASRC are not some racist's caricature of impoverished or dangerous people from a far-flung land. They include the doctor who speaks nine

halloumitracksuit This made me so happy. Just took an Uber and the man who picked me up, Syed was a person seeking #asylum who came to the #ASRC back in 2010 seeking our help, which we gave. He was like "I remember you" and my heart was like bursting 😍😍 He's now an Australian Citizen and is doing great! Was telling me how he sponsors a child in Somalia to go to school as he wants to give back. He wanted a selfie so here it is. 💚💚💚💚

With Syed, my Uber driver one morning earlier this year, who had sought the ASRC's help back in 2010. I was so delighted by this chance encounter with him that I shared it on Instagram.

languages, the young man who is now studying law and business after arriving by boat as an unaccompanied child without a word of English. They are everyday mums and dads willing to do anything, often the jobs no Australians will touch, just to put food and dignity on the table for their families. They are my heroes, my role models and this nation's future.

Immigrants and refugees have always been important to Australia's story, in building the Snowy Mountains Scheme, in helping to fight for our own freedoms, and in representing our country abroad, and not just in sport but across so many industries. Many of our refugees have become distinguished Australians, such as the Governor of South Australia, His Excellency Hieu Van Le AC, and the world-leading surgeon Dr Munjed Al Muderis, who makes it possible for our amputee diggers to walk again. But refugees shouldn't have to be exceptional to get our protection. No one expects that of you in return for your freedom and safety.

I'm disappointed that as a refugee movement we haven't been able to force the Labor Party or the Coalition to truly justify, defend or explain themselves. And the truth is we have been far too reactive instead of proactive with our vision of what an alternative, humane and compassionate approach should look like. At times we too have been lost at sea.

But there is no denying the fact that the politics and debate have been one-dimensional, which diminishes us all. You cannot pretend to care about the drownings of refugees at sea while punishing those who don't drown. A real debate would have been anchored in questions and moral challenges to our nation, such as: How do we save more lives? How many refugees can we save? What would be possible if, instead of wasting billions on offshore detention, we spent that money on integrating and settling refugees? We might then ask: Why don't we safely settle refugees en masse from Indonesia? Why don't we invest in community-based settlements, and let people work and give back what they've received? We might ask: How do we get our neighbours to share humanitarian obligations based on mutual respect, engagement and investment in capacity and human rights? How do we provide dignity and human rights in our region to refugees in transit? These are all questions worth asking and worth considering how best to answer.

Some days it can be hard to keep fighting the good fight, but most mornings when I go into work I say something to our volunteers, a little like a pep talk, for me as well as for them. 'It's in the darkness when you need to burn the brightest,' I might say. 'That's why it matters that you're here, and why we can't surrender hope. Not now, not ever.' And then the morning comes around to

REFUGEES DON'T NEED TO BE SAVED; THEY HAVE ALREADY SAVED THEMSELVES. THEY DON'T NEED OTHERS SPEAKING FOR THEM; THEY NEED THEIR VOICES TO BE HEARD.

lunchtime and I know I can't lose hope. Who could possibly lose hope on seeing these people sitting down to eat with each other with huge grins on their faces? And seeing their smiles while knowing that they have forsaken their home, their family, their job, often in fear for their lives, to find safety and to try to start over again. How brightly hope burns. Refugees are true heroes and they always have been. No one is more resilient. Refugees don't need to be saved; they have already saved themselves. They don't need others speaking for them; they need their voices to be heard.

16

THE POWER OF HOPE

It's time for me to come clean. Some months ago I was lying in a flimsy blue hospital gown with electrodes taped to all parts of my upper body, about to have an MRI. I was terrified. My doctor thought I was having heart problems. What if this is it? I asked myself. What if I'm dying right now?

Also around that time my long-term relationship was unravelling, leaving me heartbroken. Six years. I was devastated. I felt that my final chance for happiness, for my life partner and for children had slipped out of my hands once and for all. There's no question I was feeling especially vulnerable. And then to make matters worse, washing over me were all my negative childhood thoughts – that I was meant to be alone forever – which at that moment seemed to be coming true.

And to compound things even further, steadily over the previous months my weight had ballooned and was now sitting at a frightening 145 kilograms. Once again I had turned to food – to cope, to hurt myself, to punish myself, to hide within myself. I was so ashamed to have gained so much weight in my relationship, and so guilty to have done that to my partner. Food had always been my trusted refuge, and it was how I coped with feeling overwhelmed, anxious and depressed. In reality, though, I knew I was not nurturing my body but wreaking self-sabotage. So here is clear proof that in spite of all my positive words and encouragement to embrace our fears, I know with all my heart how difficult it can be to always maintain this. We can slip up and let other things take us over. That's part of being human, I guess. We are all constant works in progress – always evolving, making mistakes, losing our way, finding it again – and that's what makes us beautiful. We are fragile and strong, unpredictable and certain, hopeful and lost, often all at the same time.

It had all been something of a perfect storm for me, but things had to change, and fast. I knew that for certain once my concerned doctor sat me down. 'You sound like you have the heart of a seventy-year-old in a forty-four-year-old's body,' he said. 'You're heading for a heart attack.'

I flew into action.

WE ARE FRAGILE
AND STRONG,
UNPREDICTABLE
AND CERTAIN,
HOPEFUL AND
LOST, OFTEN
ALL AT THE
SAME TIME.

Soon, my weekday afternoons were spent in beige waiting rooms with men in their late sixties and seventies and well-thumbed copies of *Women's Weekly*. How the hell am I here with these much older men? I asked myself. My doctor had thought I might have chronic heart disease, as I kept exhibiting symptoms consistent with it such as constant chest pains, sharp pains that wouldn't go away, a shortness of breath and the most terrible fatigue that I simply could not shake. A year earlier I had fought off pneumonia and had been prescribed tablets to slow my heart down. I had asked the chemist how long I'd have to take them. 'Forever,' he had matter-of-factly replied at the time.

One afternoon while visiting my GP, I worried that I was having a heart attack right then and there, and he quickly did an ECG to see if I needed to go to Emergency. That was the first of months of tests to get to the bottom of what was happening.

As well as all these personal crises, it had been an incredibly tough year for work and I felt I had absolutely nothing left to give. What do you do when you're running on empty emotionally and physically? As a leader, naturally you feel you need to lead by example, showing people a way through these problems, reassuring them that everything will be okay. And I honestly felt that my personal needs paled in comparison to the crisis facing refugees. Each day I saw people without a roof over their heads, without food or income; people who had suffered years of being in limbo and who were under constant threat of being deported to face possible torture and death. My needs couldn't compete with those of these people, that would be selfish and self-centred of me. So they didn't.

I'm also a social worker and lawyer, so it seemed reasonable to think that I could work this out by myself and not to have to ask for help. (Caregivers are, ironically, the worst people at caring for themselves.) I had spent decades counselling others through crisis, teaching healthy boundaries, watching for signs of vicarious trauma and burnout, but I denied that I was struggling.

No one at work knew my long-term relationship was falling apart, or how potentially serious my health issues were (though people were worried), but I couldn't afford to fall apart; too much depended on me not doing so. If I lost it, if I broke, what message would I be sending to others who looked to me for hope? I can see now that I had lost the ability to distinguish how much of this was my take on things and how much was what people expected of me. I had lost sight of where one started and the other finished.

So I'm sure you can imagine that at that time the last thing I wanted to do was write this book, especially because I was in real despair. I was scared. I thought I had nothing positive to share with you, nothing to make you feel a little less alone in this world, nothing to give you comfort in times of chaos or inspiration in your times of despair. But then I thought that *was* the book – this, this messy darkness that so many of us have experienced. Perhaps I could try to show you that where there is darkness there is also light, and that where there is despair there is also hope.

I'm sure that none of this is what you were expecting of me. Perhaps you see me as someone confident and in control. And I *am* confident, self-assured, in control, resilient and full of hope at times. But how I got there, how I can do those things, to be that light, hope and strength for people, that comes from struggle and suffering. That's how it's authentic, because I'm living, aching, breathing and feeling all I say and do with every inch of my being.

I hope that in knowing this, you might also decide to address the hurt or doubt or insecurity you might be burdened with. And you can rise above it. You can be powerful even when you feel helpless or lost.

Over the past months I had to take stock and again face my fears. And I did ask for help and regularly saw a psychologist over six months to help support and guide me through my mess. And I realised I had started to repeat self-destructive behaviours from my twenties and earlier, and had been punishing myself. It's so exhausting to repeat our mistakes over and over again, and to beat ourselves up for retreating back into old harmful patterns. It seems that no matter how hard you might try to be 'normal', 'make sense' and 'fit in', it comes apart. And once again I had to let go of that expectation of ever trying to be normal, to make sense or fit in. Once again I had to let go of punishing myself for being vulnerable and messy, and to recognise that it's essential that I be authentic and who I truly am.

So once again I've had to stare down my many fears – of being alone, of losing myself in work and food, of an early grave. I refuse to let them define me any longer, or to hold me hostage. Now I start each day with words of patience, kindness and encouragement: 'Kon, it's okay, I know you're not where you want to be yet but you're getting there. I'm proud of you. Be gentle, keep going, you'll get there.'

I am at a new crossroads but this is one of my own conscious design. I don't want to find my honour in pushing through things any more; I don't want to be a martyr at the cost of my health or my happiness. As men we get taught destructive messages that real men don't stop, real men just keep going, they ignore their health, they put work first, they don't show emotion or weakness. And the minute you stop following these rules your competency, ability, talent and commitment are questioned. Is it any wonder we condemn so many men to an early grave from heart attacks, strokes and heart disease when we send men these messages every day? We need to unlearn these messages as men; they are literally killing us.

I want all the beautiful and good things I do now to come from a place of hope and optimism, from having confidence in myself and my life. How can I be a genuine beacon for hope and change if I can't feel it for myself too? I genuinely want my self-worth and self-love to at be the centre of all that I do. So in relearning these lessons and taking small steps, I am once again heading in the right direction.

My health is coming back slowly but it will take time. I'm no longer taking those tablets to slow my heart down. There are no more chest pains or afternoons spent at the doctor, no more electrodes attached to my chest that leave bald patches afterwards and no more flimsy blue hospital gowns. The results of the MRI tests showed that my heart was in fact in terrific shape. All of the symptoms had been psychological – all that pressure, depression and stress. I was overcome with relief but still troubled that my work and lack of any work–life balance had brought me to such a crisis. And so I made other changes in my life, too.

My new daily routine includes at least two hours of exercise and only good, nourishing food. I'm spending much more time in the kitchen as I love to cook, especially Greek food (with a little halloumi – you need some cheekiness in your cooking!). But I have worked on no longer using food as an emotional crutch, replacing it with other activities that are nurturing to me. I'm spending more time with my family and getting lost picking olives from my olive trees, making bread in my wood-fired oven and getting my hands deep into the soil of my garden. I'm also enjoying being an uncle to my gorgeous nephew, Leo – it's such a gift – and I'm spending more time with my wonderful friends. I'm blessed with so many gorgeous people in my life who get me, and who support me as I do them.

I have lost 21 kilograms in sixteen weeks. Sure, there's still more to go but I know I will get there. I also know I'm worthwhile and lovable no matter what weight I am. We all are. I'm proud of myself and believe I'm worth the effort. I now get up two hours before I leave each day, giving myself time for that love, just for me. And it feels so good!

I have wound back to four days a week at work, which seems reasonable after almost seventeen years. I also reckon I have twenty-plus more years of fighting the good fight, so I want to be at my best. I'm learning to say no to many of the countless requests I get or to suggest someone else so they have a chance to shine, and I don't feel guilty about it.

And now I'm single, which is scary in your forties. But that's okay. I know I'm in the best place emotionally that I have ever been to make my next serious relationship succeed. I know myself better now than I ever have. I know what I want from a partner and what I will bring to our relationship, and that feels like progress. However, it is going to take from me a willingness to put my relationship first before my work (something I have been poor at doing in the past) and be truly present. I have to own my part in this and make sure that the best of me, my heart, my energy is not taken by work but rather is there for my partner, my family and friends.

We're all fighting our own battles, many unknown even to those who are closest to us. I want you to know that you're not alone and that there is a way forward, a way through this. Asking for help is strength, being vulnerable is brave, and telling people you're not okay and letting them help you until you're ready to stand on your own two feet makes very good sense.

We're all capable of the most incredible resilience, empathy, compassion and connection, qualities that spring from the very things that are meant to be our weaknesses. We're not weak because we suffer and doubt ourselves – we're human. We all deserve to love and to be loved. We deserve forgiveness, patience, self-love and perspective. We deserve to start again, rebuild our lives, accept our insecurities and use them to help drive us to be our best selves. Go gently and with passion, purpose and hope.

Hope is only exhausted if we forsake ourselves. No one else can take it from us. It's both our sanctuary and our destiny to live a life with love, belonging, connection and community. Love yourself, for a life with self-love is a life fully realised and experienced. These are the lives we all deserve.

GO GENTLY AND WITH PASSION, PURPOSE AND HOPE.

EPILOGUE

Some final thoughts …

I hope my book gives you some comfort and solace in your darkest times by showing how we can all rise from our own ashes. I have found writing this book the most confronting thing I have done – and the most cathartic. While I was brought to tears many times, the process has been a healing one in that it allowed me to shed so much of the shame I have carried alone, as well as the silence that I have held on to for so long, for *too* long.

I know facing our trauma and fears is not easy for any of us, and that it is a daily struggle and a test of our faith in ourselves. We all feel hurt and grieve for moments and lives not lived, words not spoken and relationships not mended.

In addition, we have our own demons in our challenge to accept ourselves as being enough. I want you to know that I *do* see you: you are complete, you are worthy and deserving of love and to be loved, with all your flaws … not someday, but now, right now. I am okay that it has taken this long for me to finally do so, for I understand I have done the best I can to this point in my life, as have you.

For we are not victims but victors; we have survived. We are the dreamers. The change makers. The custodians of hope. The truth tellers, at a time where it's needed more than ever before.

It is time for me and you to tell a new story about ourselves, one that affirms and elevates us, and it is time for our country to do the same. I shared with you at the beginning of this book the deep despair I felt that late wintry Melbourne night until Mohamed picked me up in his cab and brought me back from the depths of my own darkness. I was lucky to have had that chance encounter.

However, if we believe in the power of our deeds, our values and our community, we don't need anyone else to give us that reassurance that doing what is right is worthwhile in itself. It takes real courage to not give up and that's what we all have already, whether we see it or not.

Hope is not a fool's pact; it is a pact with our best selves, the one we allow to be seen in quiet and hidden moments. It's the resilient and brave you that is holding on right now.

Hope is a pact with our true, undiluted vision of the country we can be: a thriving, inclusive democracy for all,

IT IS TIME FOR ME AND YOU TO TELL A NEW STORY ABOUT OURSELVES, ONE THAT AFFIRMS AND ELEVATES US, AND IT IS TIME FOR OUR COUNTRY TO DO THE SAME.

one with equality and justice at its very foundation and core.

I'm not asking you to believe that despair won't ever seek you out again. But when it next comes knocking at your door, respond with love for yourself and your neighbours. Speak only with words of hope and acts of compassion, for there is no room for hate and no time for compromise or fear any more.

One day our love, our sense of community and our unity will triumph. That day is coming soon – I can feel it – if we stand and work together. Love and care together. Dream and fight together.

I promise you.

Me in front of the Malcolm Fraser mural (created by the graffiti artist Heesco) that adorns the side of the ASRC in Footscray, 2017. © Kim Landy

HOW THINGS CAN CHANGE

BE THE BEST YOU

I want you to close your eyes, take a big deep breath and imagine the best you. What is the life you live? The values and work you're known for? The relationships you have? The principles you stand for? What is the legacy you're leaving, not just for your family but the community around you?

How far are you right now from that best you? What is preventing you from realising it? What is the power you need to transform your life? What are the small steps you can take tomorrow to begin it? What baggage from your emotional suitcase do you need to empty? What soundtrack do you need to change from that well-worn record that plays your story back to you each time?

Each year we have a check-up with our doctor, so now I want to ask you to do an 'Am I living an authentic life?' check-up. I want you to write down or draw what your life looks like right now. Leave nothing out and ask yourself, Is there balance for me? Is there meaning for me?

If you're not living an authentic life, it will come out in psychosomatic ways, as it did with me. You will feel it in raised anxiety levels, you will feel it in weight gain, lack of exercise, depression, trouble sleeping, aggression, lack of interest, lack of motivation and feeling as if you're an observer of your own life.

Where do your heart, time, energy and creative abilities go right now? How much time do you spend on nurturing yourself and your community right now? What is the one thing you're most proud of outside of your family? Is it something you do, a value you lead with, the person you try to be each day, a legacy you're building, or is it a thing, a possession, a status, a title that you have? No one ever asks this of us, do they?

Don't *settle*, in either work or your personal life. Being happy is much harder work than being miserable. Being happy means being present in all you do. It means taking nothing for granted, it means growing and learning after every relationship or friendship that ends, it means not being complacent in life but rather being hungry to learn and grow more. It means recognising that happiness is possible even if it comes in lots of small moments.

The best you is waiting for you. Make that first step to explore, take risks and connect with it.

LETTER TO MY EIGHTEEN-YEAR-OLD SELF

People often ask me how I created the ASRC, and whether I had planned for it to become as big as it has or to enjoy the support that it has. My answers are: I just did it, and no and no. If I had actually tried to imagine it growing to this size, I would never have started. I would have been far too terrified. And I think that's a common response from most people who have made things: if people thought too hard about these things they would talk themselves out of changing the world. Here's some advice I'd give to my eighteen-year-old self with all the life experience I have now. Perhaps it might be of use to you, too:

> You don't need to have anything figured out at eighteen, or at thirty-five. The pressure to know

what you want to do with your life and have it all sorted out is a lie. When I finished high school I missed getting into law by miles. I scraped into my first degree by one mark and then went on to become a lawyer, social worker and teacher, and hold six degrees including three masters. Nothing can stop your ambition.

Find an issue that's closest to your heart, which you can spend your life championing. If you do that you can never go wrong – that will always be you at your best. If you don't yet know what that is, take the time to explore. Try everything you're curious about, follow the feelings you're hungry for – excitement, a challenge, to be engaged, connected to something deeper than yourself – and, together with your heart and imagination, let them take you wherever they will. That's what I did when I volunteered for dozens of different charities in my twenties and thirties.

Start small and don't think too much about it. If you do you'll be overwhelmed. Just start.

Find like-minded people who get you, your passion and your vision, and whom you can trust.

Ask people for help; don't be afraid to ask. People want to help and often the biggest mistake we make is not asking at all.

Take risks. Remember, the greatest risk lies in not trying at all. In my work I always think the greatest risk is refugees dying and then I work back from there.

Be independent. People often chase the government dollar, thinking it will bring them great freedom and impact, but in reality it just imprisons you and limits your imagination and possibilities. Know your values and mission, and build and uphold a culture that embraces and celebrates and breathes and lives what you aspire to change, create and build.

Most importantly, be kind and gentle on yourself, for no one will be a fiercer critic of you than you. You are enough as you are, always. You deserve to be loved and to love yourself. When you don't believe it, live, speak and act as though you do.

HELP SHAPE THE BEST COMMUNITY

The best sort of change often happens at the grassroots level of your own local communities. It's usually bottom-up and driven by groups and passionate individuals.

Spaces of culture, dialogue and connection transform a community. A safe community often means a community with many public spaces, such as community gardens, art spaces, libraries, schools, sporting clubs, swimming pools, parks, community health centres and halls. And certainly the more engaged a community is, the safer and more prosperous it is.

There is a direct link between education and employment outcomes, and the public and social spaces people live and meet within, and their connection to culture and safety. Have you noticed how flush affluent neighbourhoods are with public spaces that include museums, galleries, cinemas, parks, inspiring street art and installations, schools and community spaces?

So let's do what we can for all communities and take action at a local level. Here are some simple things to get you started:

- Volunteer for or donate to the Asylum Seeker Resource Centre to help refugees
- Champion a Reconciliation Action Plan in your workplace
- Be the change you want to see and run for political office at any level
- Begin a community garden with friends/ neighbours to bring people together
- Build safe and inclusive spaces for people of colour, Indigenous and LGBTIQA youth in your community, schools, places of worship, workplaces, sporting and cultural spaces
- Start by acknowledging that you are gathering on the land of First Nations people every time you speak in a public forum
- Host a welcome dinner for newly arrived refugees in your community
- Volunteer at a homework club or breakfast club at your local public school

- Host an event at your workplace for Close the Gap Day
- Do a food drive for your favourite local charity or Foodbank
- Volunteer at a local animal shelter or get your next pet from one
- Visit and provide friendship to refugees imprisoned at your local immigration detention centre
- Get other men to join you in cooking breakfast for the women at your work on International Women's Day; join a Reclaim the Night rally on International Women's Day
- Start a book or board games club, or fathers/ mothers group to reduce isolation in your community
- Repurpose neglected public spaces into art, music, play and theatre spaces
- Offer free dog-walking services to frail and elderly neighbours in your street
- Lobby and campaign for better public transport, public lighting, community and art spaces, parks, playgrounds, etc, in your local area
- Set up a giving program at your workplace for a local charity
- Recycle the love by donating your pre-loved clothes and books to a charity in need

- Help cook and serve meals at a homeless shelter
- Shop at locally owned businesses where the money is more likely to stay in the community, creating local jobs and supporting family-run businesses
- Get a knitting or sewing group going to make baby clothes, scarves, gloves and blankets for communities in need during winter
- Grow your own vegetables, fruits and herbs in an organic garden, and encourage others to do the same
- Ride to work instead of driving your car to reduce pollution; put a bike rack outside your business to encourage more people to ride their bikes
- Turn unused parking lots into community gardens and parks
- Get a congregation together to visit your local federal MP to demand an end to the offshore imprisonment of refugees on Manus Island and Nauru
- Write personal letters to refugees in detention to let them know you care
- Write to governments urging them to free political prisoners
- Give blood and sign up for the Australian Organ Donor Register

- Get your council, neighbours and/or local businesses to work together to fix up rundown playgrounds, picnic benches and BBQs
- If you're a parent, join your school's Parents Association or help out at the school any way you can
- Speak up. Concerned about a local issue? Then visit, write to or call your local MP and demand real action from your political representative
- Petition for that local bike or walking path or help build one; start your own activist group on an issue you care about or run a campaign on it
- Volunteer at your local community legal centre or health centre
- Join a protest, sit-in or rally on a social justice issue close to your heart
- Boycott all Australia Day celebrations held on January 26th and instead attend a Survival Day event; support calls to Change the Date and adopt the Uluru Statement
- Create a pop-up outdoor cinema, dog park, music festival or dance space for the night to bring people together and build connections
- Crowdfund to raise money for better books, equipment and materials for your local kindergarten or library

- Hold an art exhibition, spoken word or poetry night at your local arts centre, pub or club to inspire people's imaginations and to support local arts
- Run a fundraiser in support of a local women's refuge
- Protect your local libraries from cutbacks
- Volunteer at any charity: participate, advocate and donate your skills and energy locally to strengthen your community
- Lobby your council to ensure the dignity of the homeless by providing a place for them to get a hot meal as well as available social housing and accessible public toilets and showers
- Visit the elderly through local friendship programs run by your council
- Start a conversation at work, home or school to positively reframe the conversation on refugees
- Be a Big Brother or Sister for vulnerable at-risk youth
- Buy only sweatshop-free clothes
- Protect our ABC and SBS
- Get your business to give back through corporate volunteering/sponsorship of a local charity
- Vote, be politically engaged; our democracy reflects our engagement and efforts

- Call for safe injecting rooms so we treat drug addiction as the health issue that it is
- Demand equal pay for men and women for same work in your workplace
- Become a community philanthropist by simply supporting local ideas and initiatives
- Demand more public housing, child care and better community facilities through campaigning and organising locally
- Organise a community forum on local issues of concern and invite all local political leaders, to hold them to account on where they stand
- Protect your community from over-development and demand any multi-storey developments have a minimum percentage set aside for social housing
- Organise community actions against any discrimination, be it attacks on a local mosque or over-policing of young people of colour
- If you're religious, organise a multi-faith event to bring together communities and promote inclusion and welcome for all
- Take advantage of the annual volunteer day your workplace offers and do good
- Fight climate change by campaigning against dirty coal power stations and anything that harms Mother Nature

- Recycle everything you can, compost, install a water tank, plant a tree or organise a yearly rubbish clean-up of your parks, creeks, lakes and beaches
- Bring your neighbours together through a street party or a shared garage sale for charity
- Host a local community action forum on how to tackle racism, Islamophobia, homophobia or male violence against women in your local community and bring together community leaders and groups to find solutions
- Run or attend a class at your local neighbourhood house/centre
- Demand Safe Schools programs for LGBTIQA kids at your local school
- Volunteer in remote community-controlled Indigenous communities
- Host a multicultural political, arts, film, music or community building event
- Get involved in your local Rural Australians for Refugees, Lions Club, Rotary, Girl Guides, Scouts or local sporting/arts/music/dance/theatre club or group
- Check on your elderly, sick and disabled neighbours in times of extreme weather
- Write to your local paper to raise awareness on social justice issues in your local area

- Support your local community radio station by becoming a subscriber, contributor or volunteer
- Campaign to make sure all public facilities in your community are accessible to people with disabilities
- Use your social media platforms to amplify the voices of First Nations people, people of colour, the LGBTIQA community and people with disabilities
- Create a little free library or book box/booth that could be positioned anywhere in your community; get your friends to donate their pre-loved books to it for the next generation
- Take a homeless person out for breakfast rather than just walk by
- Engage local artists and young people to create murals that will bring more warmth, colour and joy to your community
- Connect. A simple smile or a hello at your local bus stop, library or shop to a stranger or someone you don't know builds stronger communities by making everyone feel they belong
- LOVE
- CARE

Just start.

Start anywhere.

There's no right place to start, just the need to start. Each act of goodwill and kindness helps build an ecosystem of compassion that feeds the best of us and replicates itself. We often don't realise how many great skills and talents we have within us that cost us nothing to share and make us feel grateful and more meaningful in the work that we do. It's okay to start wherever you feel safe and go from there; the important thing is to start.

We have so much power within us and our own communities. The power of goodness, the power of caring, the power of raising good people, the power of being kind to yourself, the power to speak up, the power to mobilise and organise, the power of protest, the power of being a positive role model to others, the power of living your values, the power of compassion and empathy, the power to make loving and healthy choices for yourself.

We're a community first, not an economy, and we need to see money invested back into it, with better access to public transport, social housing, health, mental health and disability services. We need more free and safe accessible public spaces and supports. We need a physical and cultural environment that inspires people to dream, not to think that their fate has already been sealed for them, that is a dead-end for them.

The phrase 'Look after your own backyard' is a catch-cry for indifference. It's a call to arms of a do-nothing generation of people who seek to silence our hearts and pit the suffering of each group into a Roman amphitheatre to battle for who's the most deserving.

Don't be afraid to speak up. We all matter. We all deserve to be treated justly and with love.

The opposite of poverty is not wealth, it's justice. Let's help make things more just for all. Let's build communities of resilience and resistance, of empathy and welcome.

It's a wonderful thing to care for our community, be it by standing up for the environment, supporting a call for a treaty, championing freedom for refugees, providing a community of welcome and hope to young Australians, or demanding action to end male violence against women. We all have within us the power to make the world a kinder, fairer and better place.

Caring is not complex, empathy is not political, trying to help more people is not naive.

Surround yourself with people who get you, in whose company you don't have to shrink yourself to be accepted or censor your passion, your anger, your voice. The key is to be an active citizen and to give back; you'll always get far more from it than you give.

Create art that provokes, fosters dialogue, tells stories, humanises issues close to your heart, allows you to have a voice. Be a mentor, open up a pathway, opportunity, work experience place for someone who has lived in disadvantage and just needs a chance to contribute, grow, find their feet. We often needed someone like that ourselves; most people doing well had at some point someone who gave them a crack, saw their potential and didn't give up on them.

Vote for candidates who uphold your values, who go beyond the slogans and actually engage with their constituency, and are willing to listen and take up the real issues of local communities regardless of whether it's politically safe, expedient or popular to do so. Great leaders do what is right, not what is easy.

Show gratitude wherever you can, be humble, maintain perspective. Try to lead with love, gratitude and balance and it will take you a long way in life, for it will also help prevent hubris from getting the best of you. Embrace who you are; your identity is as important as anyone else's. Make happiness a priority, and involve yourself with music and art that inspire you.

Celebrate humanity, for our humanness is our shelter from cruelty. Our compassion is our sanctuary from indifference.

If you can, travel and get some more perspective on the world. See its wonder. Immerse yourself in the beauty of other cultures, rituals and ways. Make new friends, find people outside your safe social circles who give you fresh perspectives on life.

It's up to us as a community to raise the flag of hope and the hand of welcome to refugees. Politics has abandoned these people; let's make a promise that *we* won't. Our borders are safe; it's our humanity that is threatened. We have a huge amount of power, and it's in the interests of governments to make us believe that we don't. Our voices matter and they count. Divest, boycott, make visible. As consumers we also hold the economic power.

ONE WEEK OF CHANGE

Having an open heart, one that actually aches when you see human suffering around you, isn't easy. It can often be a real challenge, but with improved resilience and compassion I believe we can meet that challenge. At the micro level we can all make individual choices in the next week that will not only help our community but also our planet, and they will cost us nothing. These changes are just about recalibrating our day-to-day choices to fit better with our values, aspirations and desire to make a difference. In the next week you could do all the following (if you haven't already) to help your community in an instant.

REVIEW YOUR SUPER

Did you know that many super funds invest in all the kinds of things you would find abhorrent? They include the military, dirty coal-fired power plants, prisons, detention centres for refugees, and exploitation of the poor and their environments in developing countries through the corporations they have shares in. Consider swapping over to an ethical super fund. All super funds have annual reports where they have to account for where they invest your money. Changing to an ethical one takes no more than an hour to do and you can still get great returns. How are ethical super funds different? They avoid investing in anything that harms people, society, animals or the environment, and instead work to support people, sustainability and human rights.

SHOP SUSTAINABLY

Sure, ending big coal and fracking is where real transformative change can occur, but if each of us does our bit on a day-to-day basis, that change can be profound too. Let's stop using plastic bags and take our own cloth bags when shopping for groceries. Let's invest in a reusable coffee cup or eco cup instead of getting our takeaway fix in cups that can't be recycled. Don't buy pre-cut fruit and vegetables; they are less fresh and always come wrapped in plastic, which creates more waste. Stop buying processed food and frozen meals; they are bad for you, with most of their nutrients long gone, and the food miles they have travelled are off the charts. Instead, shop locally – your local fresh fruit and veg store is probably run by a local family who will then pay it forward, unlike multinationals, which will most times send their profits offshore to avoid paying tax.

BE A GRASSROOTS PATRON OF THE ARTS

You can support the arts without being rich and fancy. It often costs nothing more than your time and a few dollars. Art is so vital to any community, and a local community without art is a community without soul, without imagination, without spaces that embrace us and nurture us.

Art is a space for dialogue, a constructive avenue for releasing frustration, anger and despair about the conditions people have to endure, for telling neglected or unheard stories, for giving a forum and a voice to the marginalised, for igniting the imagination and the heart, and celebrating our curiosity, complexity and messiness as human beings.

So go to that amateur independent theatre production at your local town hall, support live music at your local pub, go to the opening night of that exhibition in some random warehouse down an alleyway, enrol in a course at your local community arts centre, go to an open-mic poetry reading at your local bar. Artists sacrifice so much and often barely live above the poverty line to create and bring their work into this world. Your support might keep them from giving up on their life's dream and passion.

EAT LESS MEAT

I've been vegetarian for more than thirty years, though I promised myself to never be dogmatic about it. Of course it's your choice but overall it's one of the best decisions I've ever made in terms of my health and wellbeing. Eating less meat is a great way to help the environment and animals. So much of our environmental destruction of land is caused by cattle and sheep bred for slaughter. So for your own sake and for the animals and the environment, try being vegetarian or at least try to reduce your meat intake to just a couple of meals a week. And while I'm at it, please don't take your children to circuses that have animals; shows like these are exploitative and dangerous for the animals.

BECOME A VOLUNTEER

On the ASRC volunteer information nights, new recruits are often anxious about whether they're skilled enough to help out. My response is that as long as you are caring, share our values and are hardworking and reliable, there's a place for you. Just consider what skills you might have that would be valuable to our local communities – finance, admin, marketing, fundraising, project management, building, design, art, cooking, carpentry, painting, IT, HR and general people skills are all much sought after.

Many charities like the ASRC also have after-hours opportunities for those who work or study full-time. So many charities also struggle to find volunteers, especially those that might be championing unpopular or unfashionable causes. Not sure where to find one? Pop into your local council and they can point you in the right direction.

HOST A FUNDRAISER

You can hold a fundraiser without it costing you a cent yet at the same time raise a couple of thousand dollars for a local charity. How? Cinemas will host a movie night for free and just take a cut of the ticket price. Stage a trivia night at a pub with a small entry fee; most pubs will give you a function room for free. Get people to sponsor you to do a run or walk for charity.

GET YOUR KIDS INVOLVED IN GIVING BACK

One of the most wonderful things you can do as a parent is get your kids involved in giving back to the community. It's one of the simplest and most powerful ways of raising the next generation of good people, of teaching them the values of empathy, compassion and community. Support them in letting them run a lemonade stand, holding a raffle or a food collection at school or writing letters to refugee children on Nauru, and also suggest that they donate their pre-loved toys to other children in need.

ENGAGE AND BRING PEOPLE WITH YOU

Do you want to have an impact or do you just want to be right? Do you want to build a movement or is winning more important? Do you want to inspire people to act or do you want them to do so temporarily through shame and guilt? Do you want to affirm and engage the best in people or do you want to feel self-righteous and judge others? If we're going to build the society and community we want, we need to bring people with us and we won't do this by talking down, by being dogmatic or by telling people everything they stand for is wrong. (I do think there might be some exceptions to this reasonableness, but I won't dwell on who they might be just now.)

We bring people with us when we show them that the change we seek from them is an affirmation of and recommitment to their values and themselves, not a rejection of them. We bring people with us when we lead with our values – that's the only thing that can triumph over fear and a disregard for facts.

We bring people with us when we use language that's aspirational and solution-focused, that builds on the best of us and celebrates it. The power of the change that is possible means reframing moral and humanitarian issues that have been politicised back into moral issues. It's about appealing to the best in each of us, recognising that most people are willing to be persuaded on any issue if given the chance, the context and the space to discuss it in a way that connects them back to our shared values.

Most people are good. No one is born racist, sexist, homophobic, Islamophobic or anti-Semitic; those prejudices are learned and they can be unlearned. If we always rush to place a label on someone before we engage with them or understand them (this isn't the same as accepting their view or conceding it's legitimate) then we've already lost them. If we want durable and sustainable change like the one we recently enjoyed with marriage equality, we need to build a change that has mass support and will survive the constant revolving door of Australian political leadership.

We need to learn to tell our stories in a way that people identify with and engage with.

We need to stop thinking that different opinions from ours are always bad. People often change their political views as they move through life, but no one wants to be targeted as bad people or wrong people, as people whose values are wrong, whose ideas are wrong. No one's going to sign up willingly after all that. Would you? I suspect not. The older people get, the more reluctant they might be to change their views, but no one wants to feel defeated and to have to own the shame of that.

So again I ask, Do we want to win the conversation or do we want to bring that person into our movement of welcome and community? At the ASRC it was tough to realise that after more than a decade of relying on myth-busting and fact sheets to win the day, all we had won over was our base. I don't mean to dismiss this, but hearing our own voice repeated back to us or being praised for it isn't going to win the day.

USE YOUR CRITICAL THINKING TO BE INFORMED

We need to stop relying on a social media algorithm to determine our news and information for the day. We need to go beyond our bubble of our base that likes and shares us and retweets us all day long, making us think that we must be changing things. We're not. Yes, we're raising awareness; yes, we're supporting and sustaining our community of allies and helping build each other's confidence to advocate and lobby more effectively, but we must go much further and reach out to the middle, to the people who could be persuaded, if we're going to create real long-term change.

We have a political 'centre right' within mainstream society that speaks of objective news as being fake, that constantly attacks our media and its independence. This at a time where journalists around the world are risking and losing their lives to report the facts.

We live in post-fact times, where we're fed a diet of misinformation and fear. Where people think having an opinion makes it a fact. Where there is now such a thing as alternative facts. We're being dumbed down on a daily basis, our attention spans and engagement reduced to nothing more than clickbait.

The sad reality is that fear trumps facts. We foolishly expect to be able to engage in a conversation where the participants are equally informed. The reality is that conversation more often than not today doesn't have the same starting point, the same facts, context, history or frame. What chance, then, do we really have in finding common ground? Next to zero.

Let's not be constantly enraged but rather informed. Let's not seek to be right, but rather to shape and build consensus. There is simply no point thinking you're right and getting on your pedestal, then looking down and seeing that no one is following you or listening to you.

I'm exhausted from watching our rage being spent on small targets. We mustn't be seduced by the idea that oppressive systems will change when individual politicians do, especially when they're not true leaders. We need to focus on dismantling the systems, structures, cultures and laws that are harming us.

LEAD WITH YOUR HEART. BE BRAVE AND TAKE RISKS

And perhaps a good place to look first at these big issues is with ourselves. There are so many moments in our lives when our values come to the fore. Think about how you feel, what you believe and how far you might go with these so we can help institute real and lasting change.

To make it easier, here's a little exercise to identify your own values. Consider the things that are most important to you and how well you embody them in relation to the following, being completely honest with yourself:

- Being kind to others
- How you engage with Mother Earth
- How you raise your children
- How you treat people when there's nothing in it for you
- How you spend your free time
- How you engage with others
- How you keep the fire burning in your belly
- How you travel
- Staying idealistic
- The businesses you support
- The conversations you have
- The day-to-day choices you make as a person
- The values you lead with
- What you share online
- Where you shop
- What you choose to spend your money on.

So lead with your heart, your sense of wonder and your imagination. Be brave and take risks. Follow your curiosity, embrace the truth that there is room for compassion for all, that our own backyard is everyone in our community, that decency and kindness aren't a competition and that we don't cherry-pick whose lives matter, because they *all* do.

CHANGE IN THE WORKPLACE

When there are more CEOs named John than there are women CEOs in Australian workplaces, we clearly have a major problem in terms of gender inequality.

I know that I'm very lucky to be in a position to help my organisation change in this regard. As a CEO I have power, and as a man I have power; and as far as I'm concerned that means I have a moral and ethical duty to lead by example. We will only have real change when we men are willing to give up some of our male privilege in the interests of fairness and justice. We become better men for it, and we create better workplaces and communities, too, when women are at the table with us as equals, as is their human right to be.

Here are the simple commitments that I make now, and that any male or female CEO could make tomorrow to improve the gender balance, equity and diversity at their company:

1. Boycott all panels and committees that have less than 50 per cent representation of women (I have been doing this for two years now)
2. Pay parity for the same work
3. Introduce ten days' paid domestic violence leave
4. Allow workplace flexibility for women and men
5. Encourage men to take on more caring roles at home by awarding them the same twelve weeks' paid leave as new mums
6. Set a minimum 50 per cent quota of women in leadership positions
7. Institute unconscious-bias training
8. Offer leadership roles as part-time/flexible positions
9. Promote a family-friendly workplace culture
10. Invest in a week of paid Aboriginal and Torres Strait Islander ceremonial leave
11. Adapt the workplace to be accessible and equitable to women and all people with disabilities
12. Ensure a safe place for LGBTIQA staff by standing up for marriage equality publicly as a CEO and organisation
13. Restructure recruitment procedures to value cultural and social capital by ensuring that there is representation of women with lived experience

as refugees in professional roles across the organisation

14. Mentor women of colour and Indigenous women, as they are grossly underrepresented in professional workplaces due to racism and sexism
15. Organise the men at work to prepare breakfast for all the female staff, volunteers and members on International Women's Day as a gesture of organisational solidarity and support
16. Practise listening to women and not interrupting them during meetings, and actively seek out their opinions and ideas; this sends an important message that women's voices matter
17. In addition to personal leave, invest in paid carer and compassionate leave
18. Sponsor as CEO a Gender Equity Plan to be led by the women on staff
19. Ensure there are female role models across the organisation, especially in leadership roles
20. Adopt a zero-tolerance policy towards sexual harassment in the workplace and make sexual harassment awareness training mandatory across the organisation

SUGGESTED READING

The Rugmaker of Mazar-e-Sharif, Najaf Mazari and Robert Hillman, Insight Publications, 2011

The Autobiography of Malcolm X: As told to Alex Haley, Malcolm X and Alex Haley, Penguin, 1964

Refusing to Be a Man: Essays of Sex and Justice, John Stoltenberg, Meridian, 1990

Strength to Love, Martin Luther King Jr, Fortress Press, 1981

Black Looks: Race and Representation, bell hooks, South End Press, 1992

Notes of a Native Son, James Baldwin, Michael Joseph, 1964

The Colour Purple, Alice Walker, Orion, 1982

I Know Why the Caged Bird Sings, Maya Angelou, Hachette Australia, 1996

Women, Race and Class, Angela Davis, Vintage Books, 1981

Long Walk to Freedom, Nelson Mandela, Abacus, 1994

What Is the What, Dave Eggers, Vintage, 2007

Sister Outsider, Audre Lorde, Ten Speed Press, 2016

The Hate Race, Maxine Beneba Clarke, Hachette Australia, 2016

Unpolished Gem, Alice Pung, Plume, 2009

These Wild Horses, Omar Sakr, Cordite Books, 2017

Just Mercy, Bryan Stevenson, Scribe Publications, 2015

ACKNOWLEDGMENTS

The quote by Martin Luther King, Jr, 'I have decided to stick with love. Hate is too great a burden to bear' is from *A Testament of Hope: The Essential Writings and Speeches* (HarperCollins Publishers, 2003). All other quotes by Dr King used in this book are from *Strength to Love*, first published in 1963. Quotes are drawn from the edition by Fortress Press, Philadelphia, 1981.

THANK YOU

I thank all of the following incredible people for their support, loyalty, love and belief in me – that is how I am still standing and dreaming:

My sister, Nola; my mum, Sia; my later father, Leo; Dan Walls; my nephew, Leo; Kam Razmara; my niece Sia; Sherrine Clark; Heidi Abdel-Raouf; Peter McNamara; Pablo Gimenez; Ellen Roberts; Emma Fulu; Gabriella Cabezas; Mandy Ord; Alex Burt; Rachel Ball; Karina Szwaja; Jana Favero; Alisha Fernando; Anita Koochew; Viktoria Komornik; Jane Vadiveloo; Allyse Symons; Anika Nicole; Uthra Ramachandran; Annie Davis; Robyn Y. Barnard; Stacey Nitchov; Sally Szmerling; Anoushka Jeronimus; Johanna Burns; Lucy De Rjx; Ariane Beeston; Michelle Bowler; Stuart Pearce; Nahal Zebarjadi; Yoko Kamada; Neda Monshat; Pasanna Mutha-Merennege; Peter Duras; Ranjana Srivastava; Arnold Zable; Michael Short; Julian Burnside; Pamela Curr; Sister Brigid Arthur; Barney Frankland; Justin Szwaja; Gabrielle Fakhri; Patrick Lawrence; Dean Shingange; Deborah Di Natale; Dennis Paphitis; Michael Da Gama Pinto; Matthew Tutty; Ann Jorgensen; Diana Mastrantuono; Eleni Stamenitis; Ziver Talat; Jarrod Kerrins; the late Dorothy Kingston; Amal Basry; the late Malcolm Fraser; Joan Lynn; Jo Kirk; Bevan

Clark; Jill Prior; Simon Hutchinson; Jane Tewson; Nicole Azzopardi; Stephanie Henry; Mathew Kenneally; Eamonn O'Toole; Neville Segrave; Shelley Burchfield; Jay Hayward; Laura Grace; Rob Catchlove; Mike Finch; Anna Dorevitch; Desley Mather; Daisy Kiriakidis; Felicidade Lay; Woody Balfour; Camille Kumar; Lisa E. Laskaridis; Father Rod Bower; Jarrod Saul McKenna; Brad Chilcott; Senem Mallman; Mohammad Al-Khafaji; Sienna Merope; Gavin Youngman; Carl Fernando; Sutapa Kabir Howlander; Gavin Ackerly; Toby Halligan; Jillian Pattinson; Dez Wildwood; Timothy O'Leary; Kate Durham; Gary Samowitz; Lillian Kline; Dean Levitan; Ian Crawford; Mary Crook; Mim and Mike Bartlett; Petrina Turner; Suzi Carp; Greg Tucker; Tamie Fraser; Monica E. Klyscz; Craig Forsyth; Christos Tsiolkas; Ken Badenoch; Maree and David Shelmerdine; Anneke and the late Arie van Klinken; Nga Luu; Mike Sum; Rebekah Lautman; Catherine Milne for believing I had a story worth telling, Lu Sierra, Lara Wallace, Hazel Lam and the entire team at HarperCollins Australia; Melanie Ostell; the men on Manus – especially Abdul Aziz Adam, Behrouz Boochani, Walid Zazai, Ezatullah Kakar and Benham Satah; the refugees that I have had the incredible honour to know; all the extraordinary staff, volunteers, supporters and board members of the Asylum Seeker Resource Centre; and all my incredible Welfare Studies students at TAFE who took a risk with me and made the ASRC possible.